VOCABULARY LADDERS

75 Reproducible Advanced Vocabulary-Building Games, Puzzles, and Activities

PHILIP A. STEINBACHER

Edited by Dianne Draze
Editorial Assistant: Kate Sepanski
Production Design by Marjorie Parker

ISBN-13: 978-1-59363-207-6
ISBN-10: 1-59363-207-X

Prufrock Press Inc.
P.O. Box 8813
Waco, TX 76714-8813
Phone: (800) 998-2208
Fax: (800) 240-0333
http://www.prufrock.com

Table of Contents

Teacher Directions

Overview

What kind of a word is *fersevently?* Have you ever heard of an *askerphtico?* After glancing through the pages of this book you might be wondering how these words fit into a valid vocabulary program. These words, as first presented in each unit in this book, are mystery words that offer an opportunity to build on students' interest in solving puzzles to draw them into the acquisition of vocabulary words that will enrich their reading and speaking abilities.

Vocabulary Ladders: Climbing Toward Language Skills Success is a collection of 15 weekly vocabulary units that require students' use of deductive reasoning, inductive reasoning, and word analysis to solve puzzles and, in the process, develop vocabulary and spelling skills. Teachers can use *Vocabulary Ladders*:

- to completely replace the traditional weekly spelling unit for specific students,
- as supplemental vocabulary/spelling units for selected students, or
- simply as additional language arts assignments.

Additionally, the units in this book can be used as replacement units for the accelerated learner in classrooms where most students will be working on traditional spelling programs. Used as replacement units, the five daily tasks can be assigned in sequential order, with task 1 given on Monday and task 5 on Friday. One benefit of assigning task 5 at the end of the week is that it can be used as an assessment at the end of the unit while other students are taking standard spelling tests. However, teachers using the book this way should be certain that the accelerated learners are not being given *more* work than the other students, just *more challenging* work. If a gifted learner is doing five vocabulary lessons each week, the other students should be doing five vocabulary or spelling lessons each week. The idea is that these units can be used to deviate the challenge level of instruction, not the amount of instruction, for advanced learners.

Tasks do not require teacher dictation. They can be assigned as in-class work or homework and can be done individually, in pairs, or in small groups. By the time students finish the exercises in each unit, they should be able to spell each of the 10 words and have an understanding of the correct definition and usage.

Sample Unit

Task 1–Unlocking the Mystery

Objective

As students complete the first exercises in each unit they will be using logic, dictionary skills, and their existing word knowledge to place each mystery word in a grid and uncover a real word. They will also match each word with a definition.

Procedure

The initial 10 mystery words used in each unit are real words in disguise. The letters of each vocabulary word appear in correct order among the letters of the mystery word. The extra letters create a need for deductive thinking and can appear before, in between, and after the correct letters. When the mystery word is placed correctly on the ladder beneath it, the letters of the vocabulary word will appear in the open rungs on the ladder and the word will be revealed. Students may (and should) use a dictionary to help decipher the word. You may initially find it necessary to give hints about the correct placement of letters in the grid. In time, though, students should become familiar with how to slide the letters in the mystery word forward and backward in the ladder to decipher the hidden vocabulary word.

Example

sladidernings

Begin by placing the mystery word into the ladder, starting anywhere you like, seeing if the letters in the open rungs spell a word.

| s | l | a | d | i | d | e | r | n | i | n | g | s | = adiern |

Keep trying. You don't have to begin at the beginning of the ladder.

| | s | l | a | d | i | d | e | r | n | i | ngs | = slaide |

Letters can "hang off" either end of the ladder, either before or after the ladder actually starts, as long as the letters stay in the original order.

| s | l | a | d | i | d | e | r | n | i | n | g | s | = didrni |

With experimentation, a word that makes sense will appear in the open rungs!

| s | l | a | d | i | d | e | r | n | i | n | gs | = ladder |

Once students have deciphered all the vocabulary words, they should use a dictionary to match the words with their correct definitions.

Task 2–True or False?

Objective

This lesson gives students an opportunity to test their understanding of the meanings of words when they are used in context or when a definition is provided.

Procedure

This exercise has two variations. Sometimes students read sentences containing the vocabulary word and must determine whether it has been used correctly and in the given context. In other instances, words and definitions are provided and students must determine whether the definition correctly fits the word. After completing the true-false section of this exercise, students will select three words that were used incorrectly and write sentences using the words in the proper context. Students should complete this exercise without the use of reference materials.

Example

true Scientists often did not consider the possible **implications** of stress and its effect on the human body.

false **imply**—to state or declare something clearly

Task 3–Parts of Speech

Objective

Students will gain more knowledge of how the vocabulary words are used in written and spoken language by identifying the part of speech and writing their own original sentences for the words.

Procedure

Students identify the part of speech of each of the week's vocabulary words and then use the words in original sentences. A bonus to task 3 has students exploring the words as other parts of speech.

Example

Word	Part of Speech	Your Sentence
nullify	*verb*	*The board's vote <u>nullified</u> their previous decision.*

Task 4–Antonyms and Synonyms

Objective

Students will be able to call on their knowledge of the words' meanings to identify an antonym for each word and then to supply a synonym. By discovering words with similar meanings, students will be exposed to additional words they can incorporate into their vocabulary.

Procedure

This task can be particularly challenging. Ten antonyms for the 10 vocabulary words are provided. Students figure out which vocabulary word has the opposite meaning to the word listed and write it under in the middle column. Then students come up with a word (or phrase) that is synonymous with the vocabulary word and write it in the last column. You can allow students to complete task 4 with or without reference materials.

Example

Antonym	Vocabulary Word	Synonym
meek	*assertive*	*confident, firm*
comply	*disobey*	*disregard, defy, violate*
ignite	*extinguish*	*quench, eliminate, stifle*

Task 5–Test

Objective

This final task will test students' ability to spell the vocabulary words and to select the correct definition.

Procedure

This "test" is a variation of the original vocabulary ladders presented in task 1 and gives students another opportunity to be word detectives. Two consecutive letters from each of the week's vocabulary words are provided on 10 blank grids. Without the use of a word bank, students must rely on deductive reasoning and word analysis to help them fill in the missing letters and correctly spell each of the week's vocabulary words.

Example

1. | *s* | *c* | *o* | **u** | **r** | *g* | *e* | = scourge

2. | *p* | *e* | **r** | **m** | *i* | *t* | = permit

Students then demonstrate understanding of the words' meanings in one of four ways. They may be asked to do one of the following:

- match the words with their meanings,
- use the words correctly in original sentences,
- match the words with their correct antonyms or synonyms, or
- define the words by providing their own definitions.

Unit 1

Name: _____

The 10 mystery words listed below contain this week's vocabulary words. The letters of each vocabulary word appear in the correct order among the letters in the mystery word; however, extra letters have been added to camouflage the vocabulary word. The extra letters can appear before, in between, and after the correct letters. When the mystery word is placed correctly in the grid, the letters of the vocabulary word will appear in the open boxes and the word will be revealed. Write the correct vocabulary word to the right of the grid. You may use a dictionary to complete this exercise.

Example: sladidernings

| | s | l | a | d | i | d | e | r | n | i | n | g | s | = ladder |

1. albironader

abroad

2. sapendingreen

Pedigree

3. malporfitsy

lofty

4. balerfulny

baleful

5. munkicripalpy

municipal

6. citharstern

chasten

7. pendriftyne

edify

8. spinelpert

inept

Name: _____

9. fersevently

| | | | | | | | | | | | | |

fervent

10. supremiciser

| | | | | | | | | | | | | |

Peemise

Finding Meaning

Once you have deciphered all the vocabulary words, use a dictionary to help you learn their meanings. Write each word next to its correct definition.

1. _____edify_____ to instruct or to provide intellectual or moral enlightenment

2. _____lofty_____ elevated in character or spirit

3. _____municipal_____ having local self-government, restricted to one locality

4. _____Premise_____ an idea that serves as the basis for a discussion or argument

5. _____abrad_____ over a wide area, away from one's home

6. _____inept_____ lacking skill or competence; not suitable

7. _____Chasten_____ to punish in order to make better; to correct by punishment

8. _____pedigree_____ an ancestral line, the origin and history of something

9. _____fervent_____ enthusiastic, showing great feeling

10. _____baleful_____ harmful, evil, or destructive

Name: _____

Determine whether the vocabulary word in boldface is used correctly. Write true or false on the line before each sentence.

1. __F__ Everyone must be extremely careful coming **abroad**, as the boat's ramp can be quite slippery.

2. __T__ Mitzi gained power over the other girls in the group through **baleful** bullying and the intentional spreading of rumors.

3. __F__ Always make sure to **chasten** the barn door securely, especially when the wind is blowing so violently

4. __T__ Mr. Blake gave Ethyl a book that was meant to **edify** the complex biology concepts he mentioned earlier in class, but even after reading it, she was still confused.

5. __F__ All the teachers were disappointed in Mike's **fervent** work habits, and encouraged him to change if he ever expected to succeed.

6. __T__ Everyone agreed that Kathy's argument was based on a very sound **premise**.

7. __T__ It wasn't hard to believe that Trevor would achieve his **lofty** goals, because everyone knew how hard he was willing to work.

8. __F__ Parker's mother loved to indulge in a weekly **pedigree**, so she visited the spa every Thursday.

9. __T__ How could Ben have been selected class president when everyone knew he was so completely **inept**?

10. __F__ Because Aaron preferred working in ways that would benefit his own local community he decided a position with the **municipal** government would not be good for him.

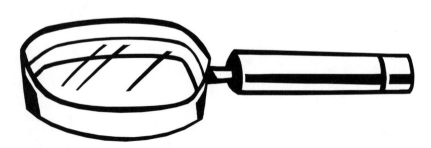

1.3 Parts of Speech

Name: _____

Identify the part of speech for each word and then use each word in an original sentence. Remember that words often can be used as more than one part of speech; if you identify a word as one part of speech, you must use it as that part of speech in your sentence.

Word	Part of Speech	Your Sentence
1. abroad	adj.	
2. baleful	verb	
3. chasten	adj	
4. edify	adj	
5. fervent	verb	
6. inept	adj	
7. lofty	adj	
8. municipal	adj	
9. pedigree	adj	
10. premise	noun	

◆ **Bonus Work**

Pick three of the vocabulary words above that can be used as more than one part of speech and use each one to write an additional sentence that shows the word being used as a different part of speech than what you used above. You may have to slightly change the form of the word to do this.

Name: _____

abroad	baleful	chasten	edify	fervent
premise	inept	lofty	municipal	pedigree

Below are antonyms for the 10 vocabulary words listed above. Next to each word in the first column, write a vocabulary word that has the opposite meaning. Then, provide a synonym (a word or phrase) in the last column for each vocabulary word.

Antonym	Vocabulary Word	Synonym
humble	lofty	arrogant
at home	abroad	overseas
conclusion	premise	assumption
able	inept	incompetent
harmless	baleful	hostile
pamper	chasten	spoil
baffle	edify	talk
global	municipal	worldly
descendants	pedigree	ancestor
indifferent	fervent	diffrent

Name: _____

Part A–Complete the Ladder

Below are ladders for each of this week's vocabulary words. Two consecutive letters from each word are given. Fill in the missing letters to correctly spell each of the vocabulary words.

1. 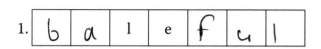 | b | a | l | e | f | u | l |

2.  | a | b | r | o | a | d |

3. 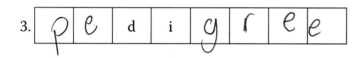 | p | e | d | i | g | r | e | e |

4. 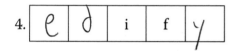 | e | d | i | f | y |

5.  | c | h | a | s | t | e | n |

6. 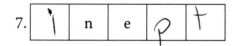 | l | o | f | t | y |

7. 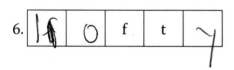 | i | n | e | p | t |

8. 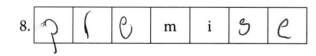 | p | r | e | m | i | s | e |

9.  | f | e | r | v | e | n | t |

10. 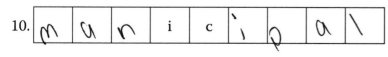 | m | u | n | i | c | i | p | a | l |

Name: _____

Part B—Show Your Understanding

Write each vocabulary word on the line next to its closest definition.

1. _____inept_____ lacking skill or competence

2. _____municpal_____ having local self-government, restricted to one locality

3. _____edify_____ to instruct and improve

4. _____baleful_____ harmful, evil, or destructive

5. _____abroad_____ away from one's home

6. _____pedigree_____ an ancestral line

7. _____lofty_____ elevated in character or spirit

8. _____chasten_____ an idea that serves as the basis for a discussion or argument

9. _____fervent_____ enthusiastic

10. _____premise_____ to correct by punishment

Unit 2

Name: _____

The 10 mystery words listed below contain this week's vocabulary words. The letters of each vocabulary word appear in the correct order among the letters in the mystery word; however, extra letters have been added to camouflage the vocabulary word. The extra letters can appear before, in between, and after the correct letters. When the mystery word is placed correctly in the grid, the letters of the vocabulary word will appear in the open boxes and the word will be revealed. Write the correct vocabulary word to the right of the grid. You may use a dictionary to complete this exercise.

Example: sladidernings

| s | l | a | d | i | d | e | r | n | i | n | g | s | = ladder |

1. macorindy

acrid

2. scarndild

candid

3. odregrandes

degrade

4. pepintraile

entail

5. loepenireant

lenient

6. moistigante

mitigate

7. suspeaceton

Peace or peact

8. tarencosils

recoil

Name: _____

9. askerphtico

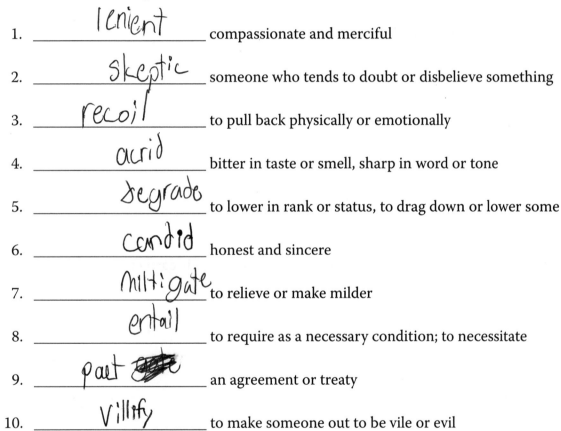

Skeptic

10. civiloifry

vivify

Finding Meaning

Once you have deciphered all the vocabulary words, use a dictionary to help you learn their meanings. Write each word next to its correct definition.

1. _____lenient_____ compassionate and merciful

2. _____skeptic_____ someone who tends to doubt or disbelieve something

3. _____recoil_____ to pull back physically or emotionally

4. _____acrid_____ bitter in taste or smell, sharp in word or tone

5. _____degrade_____ to lower in rank or status, to drag down or lower some

6. _____candid_____ honest and sincere

7. _____miltigate_____ to relieve or make milder

8. _____entail_____ to require as a necessary condition; to necessitate

9. _____pact_____ an agreement or treaty

10. _____villify_____ to make someone out to be vile or evil

Name: _____

Determine whether the definition for each vocabulary word is correct. Write true or false on the line before each word.

1. __T__ **candid**—genuine, truthful

2. __T__ **mitigate**—to relieve or make milder

3. __F__ **acrid**—having a strong, pleasant fragrance

4. __T__ **recoil**—to pull back physically or emotionally

5. __T__ **degrade**—to lower in rank or status, to drag down or lower someone

6. __F__ **pact**—completed, requiring no further action

7. __F__ **lenient**—enthusiastic, avid

8. __T__ **entail**—to require or imply as necessary

9. __F__ **skeptic**—someone who believes everything he hears

10. __F__ **vilify**—to hurt someone's feelings, to insult someone

Choose three words that you indicated had incorrect definitions and write their correct definitions.

Vocabulary Word   **Definition**

Vilify _____   ___To make evil_____

_____   _____

_____   _____

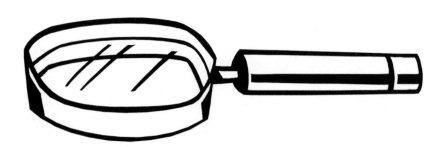

Name: _____

Identify the part of speech for each word and then use each word in an original sentence. Remember that words often can be used as more than one part of speech; if you identify a word as one part of speech, you must use it as that part of speech in your sentence.

Word	Part of Speech	Your Sentence
1. acrid	adj	
2. candid	~~verb~~ adj.	
3. degrade	~~adj.~~ verb	
4. entail	verb ~~adj.~~	
5. lenient	~~noun~~ adj	
6. mitigate	verb	
7. pact	noun	
8. recoil	verb	
9. skeptic	noun	
10. vilify	verb	

◆ **Bonus Work**

Pick three of the vocabulary words above that can be used as more than one part of speech and use each one to write an additional sentence that shows the word being used as a different part of speech than what you used above. You may have to slightly change the form of the word to do this.

Name: _____

| acrid | candid | degrade | entail | lenient |
| mitigate | pact | recoil | skeptic | vilify |

Below are antonyms for the 10 vocabulary words listed above. Next to each word in the first column, write a vocabulary word that has the opposite meaning. Then, provide a synonym (a word or phrase) in the last column for each vocabulary word.

Antonym	Vocabulary Word	Synonym
compliment	degrade	hate
insincere	candid	
disagreement	pact	agreement
strict	lienient	lax
glorify	vilify	corrupt
believer	skeptic	skeptical
fragrant	acrid	aroma
intensify	mitigate	simplify
move toward	recoil	retaliate
not be necessary	entail	necessary

Vocabulary Ladders © Prufrock Press Inc. This page may be photocopied or reproduced with permission for student use.

Name: _____

Part A–Complete the Ladder

Below are ladders for each of this week's vocabulary words. Two consecutive letters from each word are given. Fill in the missing letters to correctly spell each of the vocabulary words.

1. | d | e | g | r | a | d | e |

2. | p | a | c | t |

3. | l | e | n | i | e | n | t |

4. | a | c | r | i | d |

5. | c | a | n | d | i | d |

6. | m | i | t | i | g | a | t | e |

7. | s | k | e | p | t | i | c |

8. | v | i | l | i | f | y |

9. | r | e | c | o | i | l |

10. | e | n | t | a | i | l |

Name: _____

Part B—Show Your Understanding

Use each of the 10 vocabulary words correctly in an original sentence.

1. _____

   _____

2. _____

   _____

3. _____

   _____

4. _____

   _____

5. _____

   _____

6. _____

   _____

7. _____

   _____

8. _____

   _____

9. _____

   _____

10. _____

   _____

Unit 3

Name: _____

The 10 mystery words listed below contain this week's vocabulary words. The letters of each vocabulary word appear in the correct order among the letters in the mystery word; however, extra letters have been added to camouflage the vocabulary word. The extra letters can appear before, in between, and after the correct letters. When the mystery word is placed correctly in the grid, the letters of the vocabulary word will appear in the open boxes and the word will be revealed. Write the correct vocabulary word to the right of the grid. You may use a dictionary to complete this exercise.

Example: sladidernings

| | s | l | a | d | i | d | e | r | n | i | n | g | s | = ladder |

1. gafoilbiles

2. tranceutaen

3. modlilifry

4. strawndrey

5. scabajercot

6. famutoilane

7. dielungest

8. pentvenliop

Name: _____

9. tresclisuses

10. shrubatiles

Finding Meaning

Once you have deciphered all the vocabulary words, use a dictionary to help you learn their meanings. Write each word next to its correct definition.

1. _____ an overflow or surge

2. _____ a fault or shortcoming

3. _____ cheap, showy, tasteless

4. _____ sharp, severe, or finely tuned

5. _____ to enclose, surround, or cover

6. _____ a hermit or loner

7. _____ understated or delicate

8. _____ to appease or calm down

9. _____ useless, pointless

10. _____ hopeless or miserable

Name: _____

Determine whether the vocabulary word in boldface is used correctly. Write
true or false on the line before each sentence.

1. _____ Everything about Heather's appearance was **tawdry**, from the bright
colors of her clothing to her cheap, flashy jewelry.

2. _____ Becca realized it was **futile** to try to argue with her parents about going to the
game once they had made up their minds.

3. _____ Jason always enjoyed visiting with his grandmother, whose positive
thinking filled him with **abject** optimism.

4. _____ It was true that Danny could be somewhat of a **recluse**, because often he felt
the need to spend time by himself.

5. _____ Because Mr. Taylor's class was excited about the project, they were able to
come up with a **deluge** of great ideas.

6. _____ Joe had many good qualities, but his greatest **foible** was his ability to
make everyone feel welcome.

7. _____ Rob had an **acute** sense of direction, and his family always teased him
about getting lost.

8. _____ The Mauna Loa volcano showed sudden, violent activity and was easily
able to **envelop** the surrounding land in hot gaseous lava.

9. _____ Jeff constantly left dozens of notes about his birthday in Roberta's
locker, believing that the **subtle** approach was the surest way to get good
presents.

10. _____ Kalei found that the best way to **mollify** Tanner after a disagreement
was to keep reminding him how she was right and he was wrong.

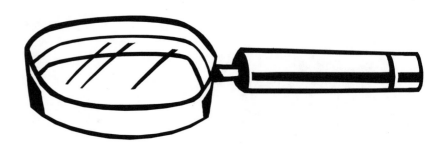

Name: _____

Identify the part of speech for each word and then use each word in an original sentence. Remember that words often can be used as more than one part of speech; if you identify a word as one part of speech, you must use it as that part of speech in your sentence.

Word	Part of Speech	Your Sentence
1. abject	_____	_____
2. acute	_____	_____
3. deluge	_____	_____
4. envelop	_____	_____
5. foible	_____	_____
6. futile	_____	_____
7. mollify	_____	_____
8. recluse	_____	_____
9. subtle	_____	_____
10. tawdry	_____	_____

◆ **Bonus Work**

Pick three of the vocabulary words above that can be used as more than one part of speech and use each one to write an additional sentence that shows the word being used as a different part of speech than what you used above. You may have to slightly change the form of the word to do this.

Name: _____

abject	acute	deluge	envelop	foible
futile	mollify	recluse	subtle	tawdry

Below are antonyms for the 10 vocabulary words listed above. Next to each word in the first column, write a vocabulary word that has the opposite meaning. Then, provide a synonym (a word or phrase) in the last column for each vocabulary word.

Antonym	Vocabulary Word	Synonym
obvious	_____	_____
moderate	_____	_____
tasteful	_____	_____
productive	_____	_____
drought	_____	_____
enrage	_____	_____
strength	_____	_____
hopeful	_____	_____
socialite	_____	_____
uncover	_____	_____

3.5 Test

Name: _____

Part A–Complete the Ladder

Below are ladders for each of this week's vocabulary words. Two consecutive letters from each word are given. Fill in the missing letters to correctly spell each of the vocabulary words.

1. | | o | l | | | | |

2. | | | | | l | e |

3. | | o | i | | | |

4. | | e | l | | | |

5. | | | | e | c | |

6. | | | c | l | | | |

7. | | c | u | | |

8. | | | | e | l | | |

9. | | a | w | | | |

10. | | | b | t | | |

Name: _____

Part B–Show Your Understanding

Listed below are antonyms for five vocabulary words and synonyms for five vocabulary words. Identify which vocabulary word is related to the antonym or synonym and write it next to the word.

Antonym	Vocabulary Word
1. enrage	_____
2. strength	_____
3. hopeful	_____
4. dull	_____
5. tasteful	_____

Synonym	Vocabulary Word
6. pointless	_____
7. flood	_____
8. hermit	_____
9. cover	_____
10. delicate	_____

Unit 4

Name: _____

The 10 mystery words listed below contain this week's vocabulary words. The letters of each vocabulary word appear in the correct order among the letters in the mystery word; however, extra letters have been added to camouflage the vocabulary word. The extra letters can appear before, in between, and after the correct letters. When the mystery word is placed correctly in the grid, the letters of the vocabulary word will appear in the open boxes and the word will be revealed. Write the correct vocabulary word to the right of the grid. You may use a dictionary to complete this exercise.

Example: sladidernings

| s | l | a | d | i | d | e | r | n | i | n | g | s | = ladder |

1. arkisnedliners

2. egrianunite

3. effiorntest

4. arvioglurter

5. pellsundie

6. semealigion

7. bonivearist

8. eustoalidress

Name: _____

9. pallauchinder

10. crinampedell

Finding Meaning

Once you have deciphered all the vocabulary words, use a dictionary to help you learn their meanings. Write each word next to its correct definition.

1. _____ easily understood, clear

2. _____ dignified, serious, unadventurous

3. _____ to stop or obstruct

4. _____ to evade or escape from by the use of cleverness

5. _____ a strong point; something a person does well

6. _____ the popular fashion or style

7. _____ to encourage or stimulate; ignite

8. _____ to speak evil of; to slander

9. _____ thin and bony; beaten down

10. _____ open; not hidden or concealed

Name: _____

Determine whether the definition for the vocabulary word is correct. Write true or false on the line before each word.

1. _____ **malign**—to make harmful or untrue statements about

2. _____ **forte**—something in which someone excels

3. _____ **kindle**—a handle or stick that yarn is wrapped around

4. _____ **impede**—to obstruct the progress of

5. _____ **vogue**—that which is popular or fashionable

6. _____ **staid**—remaining longer than you are welcome

7. _____ **overt**—complete or finished

8. _____ **lucid**—profitable

9. _____ **elude**—an intermission or a pause

10. _____ **gaunt**—underweight and haggard

Choose three words that you indicated had incorrect definitions and write their correct definitions.

Vocabulary Word   **Definition**

_____   _____

_____   _____

_____   _____

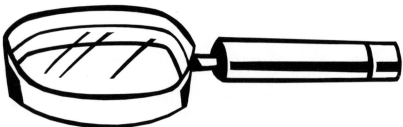

Name: _____

Identify the part of speech for each word and then use each word in an original sentence. Remember that words often can be used as more than one part of speech; if you identify a word as one part of speech, you must use it as that part of speech in your sentence.

Word	Part of Speech	Your Sentence
1. elude	_____	_____
2. forte	_____	_____
3. gaunt	_____	_____
4. impede	_____	_____
5. kindle	_____	_____
6. lucid	_____	_____
7. malign	_____	_____
8. overt	_____	_____
9. staid	_____	_____
10. vogue	_____	_____

◆ **Bonus Work**
 Pick three of the vocabulary words above that can be used as more than one part of speech and use each one to write an additional sentence that shows the word being used as a different part of speech than what you used above. You may have to slightly change the form of the word to do this.

Name: _____

elude	forte	gaunt	impede	kindle
lucid	malign	overt	staid	vogue

Below are antonyms for the 10 vocabulary words listed above. Next to each word in the first column, write a vocabulary word that has the opposite meaning. Then, provide a synonym (a word or phrase) in the last column for each vocabulary word.

Antonym	Vocabulary Word	Synonym
confused	_____	_____
unpopularity	_____	_____
plump	_____	_____
encounter	_____	_____
advance	_____	_____
weakness	_____	_____
extinguish	_____	_____
hidden	_____	_____
praise	_____	_____
adventurous	_____	_____

Name: _____

Part A—Complete the Ladder

Below are ladders for each of this week's vocabulary words. Two consecutive letters from each word are given. Fill in the missing letters to correctly spell each of the vocabulary words.

1. | | | e | r | |

2. | | | | e | d | |

3. | | | r | t | |

4. | | | | d | e |

5. | | | u | n | |

6. | | a | l | | | |

7. | | o | g | | |

8. | | | c | i | |

9. | | | n | d | | |

10. | | | | i | d |

Name: _____

Part B—Show Your Understanding

Write each vocabulary word and provide a short definition.

Vocabulary Word	**Definition**

1. _____   _____

                 _____

2. _____   _____

                 _____

3. _____   _____

                 _____

4. _____   _____

                 _____

5. _____   _____

                 _____

6. _____   _____

                 _____

7. _____   _____

                 _____

8. _____   _____

                 _____

9. _____   _____

                 _____

10. _____   _____

                 _____

Unit 5

Name: _____

The 10 mystery words listed below contain this week's vocabulary words. The letters of each vocabulary word appear in the correct order among the letters in the mystery word; however, extra letters have been added to camouflage the vocabulary word. The extra letters can appear before, in between, and after the correct letters. When the mystery word is placed correctly in the grid, the letters of the vocabulary word will appear in the open boxes and the word will be revealed. Write the correct vocabulary word to the right of the grid. You may use a dictionary to complete this exercise.

Example: sladidernings

| | s | l | a | d | i | d | e | r | n | i | n | g | s | = ladder |

1. abiolisatera

2. evearbloste

3. speersitaloys

4. pimsingules

5. meschouffy

6. vandroiditer

7. sapprosents

8. stairiflagle

Name: _____

9. exaplimoist

10. dripliater

Finding Meaning

Once you have deciphered all the vocabulary words, use a dictionary to help you learn their meanings. Write each word next to its correct definition.

1. _____ to support or prop up

2. _____ something of little value, a small amount

3. _____ to expand or become wider

4. _____ skillful or experienced

5. _____ using an excessive number of words

6. _____ to mix or bring together

7. _____ ordinary speech or writing

8. _____ to use selfishly or for profit

9. _____ to mock or make fun of; to jeer at

10. _____ danger, exposure to harm

Name: _____

Determine whether the vocabulary word in boldface is used correctly. Write true or false on the line before each sentence.

1. _____ As the room gets darker you will notice that your pupils **dilate** a great deal to take in more light.

2. _____ Nadia was comfortable in all situations, because she was **adroit** at starting conversations with almost anyone.

3. _____ Mary Anne hoped her cousin would play some dance music at the party so she could show all her friends how well she could do the **mingle**.

4. _____ Peggy was able to recite the entire pledge **verbose**, not missing a single word or phrase.

5. _____ William Shakespeare is considered one of the greatest poets because of his many contributions to **prose** writing.

6. _____ Things looked inexplicably calm on the lower deck of the ship, but Julian knew he was still in great **peril**.

7. _____ Businesses in some countries have been known to **exploit** children, making them work in factories and warehouses at very young ages.

8. _____ Mrs. Babbitt was afraid her guests might **scoff** her beautiful new dining room floor and asked them to remove their shoes before entering her home.

9. _____ Ross expected a large pay increase when he was promoted, but his new salary was just a **trifle** more than his previous salary.

10. _____ Ethan's family was happy that he had won the regional spelling bee, because it really helped to **bolster** his confidence.

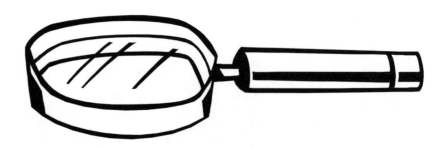

Name: _____

Identify the part of speech for each word and then use each word in an original sentence. Remember that words often can be used as more than one part of speech; if you identify a word as one part of speech, you must use it as that part of speech in your sentence.

Word	Part of Speech	Your Sentence
1. adroit	_____	_____
2. bolster	_____	_____
3. dilate	_____	_____
4. exploit	_____	_____
5. mingle	_____	_____
6. peril	_____	_____
7. prose	_____	_____
8. scoff	_____	_____
9. trifle	_____	_____
10. verbose	_____	_____

◆ **Bonus Work**

Pick three of the vocabulary words above that can be used as more than one part of speech and use each one to write an additional sentence that shows the word being used as a different part of speech than what you used above. You may have to slightly change the form of the word to do this.

Name: _____

| adroit | bolster | dilate | exploit | mingle |
| peril | prose | scoff | trifle | verbose |

Below are antonyms for the 10 vocabulary words listed above. Next to each word in the first column, write a vocabulary word that has the opposite meaning. Then, provide a synonym (a word or phrase) in the last column for each vocabulary word.

Antonym	Vocabulary Word	Synonym
shrink	_____	_____
poetry	_____	_____
treat fairly	_____	_____
awkward	_____	_____
stay separate	_____	_____
weaken	_____	_____
safety	_____	_____
a lot	_____	_____
concise	_____	_____
applaud	_____	_____

Name: _____

Part A–Complete the Ladder

Below are ladders for each of this week's vocabulary words. Two consecutive letters from each word are given. Fill in the missing letters to correctly spell each of the vocabulary words.

1. | | c | o | | |

2. | | r | i | | | |

3. | | | | o | i | |

4. | | o | s | |

5. | | | s | t | | |

6. | | | o | i | |

7. | | r | i | |

8. | | l | a | | |

9. | | r | b | | | |

10. | | | g | l | |

Name: _____

Part B—Show Your Understanding

Write each vocabulary word on the line next to its closest definition.

1. _____ containing excessive words

2. _____ exposure to danger or the risk of harm or injury

3. _____ something unimportant, a little bit

4. _____ ordinary speech or writing

5. _____ to ridicule or make fun of

6. _____ to support, encourage, or prop up

7. _____ to take advantage of, use selfishly

8. _____ to mix or associate with others

9. _____ to widen or expand

10. _____ skillful or highly able

Unit 6

Name: _____

The 10 mystery words listed below contain this week's vocabulary words. The letters of each vocabulary word appear in the correct order among the letters in the mystery word; however, extra letters have been added to camouflage the vocabulary word. The extra letters can appear before, in between, and after the correct letters. When the mystery word is placed correctly in the grid, the letters of the vocabulary word will appear in the open boxes and the word will be revealed. Write the correct vocabulary word to the right of the grid. You may use a dictionary to complete this exercise.

Example: sladidernings

| | s | l | a | d | i | d | e | r | n | i | n | g | s | = ladder |

1. tinniastoes

2. pitherislope

3. gurtbrander

4. slugachenit

5. amilopoffy

6. mobatrupsen

7. popioserts

8. hainadear

Name: _____

9. stumbodule

10. leandiorstep

Finding Meaning

Once you have deciphered all the vocabulary words, use a dictionary to help you learn their meanings. Write each word next to its correct definition.

1. _____ shining, clear

2. _____ concise and brief

3. _____ to delay, interrupt, or stop

4. _____ to conquer or overpower

5. _____ not sharp; slow to understand

6. _____ existing from birth, inborn, natural

7. _____ reflecting elegance and sophistication

8. _____ the state of having dignity, self-confidence, or grace

9. _____ distant or disinterested

10. _____ to approve of or support

Name: _____

Determine whether the definition for the vocabulary word is correct. Write true or false on the line before each word.

1. _____ **poise**—showing grace and confidence

2. _____ **terse**—very tight, stressed

3. _____ **hinder**—far away, at a great distance

4. _____ **innate**—occurring naturally, inborn

5. _____ **endorse**—to decorate or adorn

6. _____ **subdue**—to owe loyalty to

7. _____ **aloof**—distant and detached

8. _____ **urbane**—living in or having to do with cities

9. _____ **obtuse**—not sharp or acute

10. _____ **lucent**—comfortable and loose

Choose three words that you indicated had incorrect definitions and write their correct definitions.

Vocabulary Word   **Definition**

_____   _____

_____   _____

_____   _____

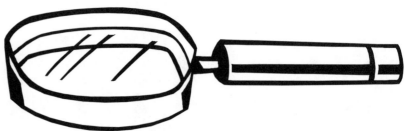

Name: _____

Identify the part of speech for each word and then use each word in an original
sentence. Remember that words often can be used as more than one part of
speech; if you identify a word as one part of speech, you must use it as that part
of speech in your sentence.

Word	Part of Speech	Your Sentence
1. aloof	_____	_____
2. endorse	_____	_____
3. hinder	_____	_____
4. innate	_____	_____
5. lucent	_____	_____
6. obtuse	_____	_____
7. poise	_____	_____
8. subdue	_____	_____
9. terse	_____	_____
10. urbane	_____	_____

◆ **Bonus Work**
   Pick three of the vocabulary words above that can be used as more than one
   part of speech and use each one to write an additional sentence that shows
   the word being used as a different part of speech than what you used above.
   You may have to slightly change the form of the word to do this.

Name: _____

| aloof | endorse | hinder | innate | lucent |
| obtuse | poise | subdue | terse | urbane |

Below are antonyms for the 10 vocabulary words listed above. Next to each word in the first column, write a vocabulary word that has the opposite meaning. Then, provide a synonym (a word or phrase) in the last column for each vocabulary word.

Antonym	Vocabulary Word	Synonym
long-winded	_____	_____
acquired	_____	_____
help	_____	_____
disapprove	_____	_____
awkwardness	_____	_____
unsophisticated	_____	_____
sharp	_____	_____
friendly	_____	_____
opaque	_____	_____
release	_____	_____

Name: _____

Part A—Complete the Ladder

Below are ladders for each of this week's vocabulary words. Two consecutive letters from each word are given. Fill in the missing letters to correctly spell each of the vocabulary words.

1. | | l | o | | |

2. | | e | r | | |

3. | | | | e | n | |

4. | | o | i | | |

5. | | u | b | | | |

6. | | | | o | r | | |

7. | | | | a | n | |

8. | | | t | u | | |

9. | | | | d | e | |

10. | | | n | a | | |

Name: _____

Part B—Show Your Understanding

Use each vocabulary word correctly in an original sentence.

1. _____

   _____

2. _____

   _____

3. _____

   _____

4. _____

   _____

5. _____

   _____

6. _____

   _____

7. _____

   _____

8. _____

   _____

9. _____

   _____

10. _____

   _____

Unit 7

Name: _____

The 10 mystery words listed below contain this week's vocabulary words. The letters of each vocabulary word appear in the correct order among the letters in the mystery word; however, extra letters have been added to camouflage the vocabulary word. The extra letters can appear before, in between, and after the correct letters. When the mystery word is placed correctly in the grid, the letters of the vocabulary word will appear in the open boxes and the word will be revealed. Write the correct vocabulary word to the right of the grid. You may use a dictionary to complete this exercise.

Example: sladidernings

| | s | l | a | d | i | d | e | r | n | i | n | g | s | = ladder |

1. renchainten

2. sabithorite

3. pleadeswary

4. steadisume

5. choviserate

6. rexpaliter

7. enturapincel

8. thisarudyne

Name: _____

9. enstustraning

10. germuslantern

Finding Meaning

Once you have deciphered all the vocabulary words, use a dictionary to help you learn their meanings. Write each word next to its correct definition.

1. _____ to take back or renounce

2. _____ to imitate in order to be equal or better

3. _____ to regard with detest

4. _____ boredom or dullness

5. _____ to glorify, praise, or honor

6. _____ a slight degree of difference or variation

7. _____ a margin of freedom of action

8. _____ resilient or enduring

9. _____ covered or not practiced openly

10. _____ to maintain or keep up

Name: _____

Determine whether the vocabulary word in boldface is used correctly. Write
true or false on the line before each sentence.

1. _____ Mark hoped Joey would grant him some **leeway** and let him decide for himself
which solution worked best.

2. _____ The biggest difficulty of living in this new climate was finding plants **hardy**
enough to survive the challenging weather.

3. _____ Melissa enjoyed many qualities of her new friendship with Anthony, even
though she felt he was very **covert** about his reasons for doing certain things.

4. _____ Will and his family understood the seriousness of his offense, but they
did not believe it was enough to **sustain** him from school.

5. _____ Casey believed the halftime show was really wonderful and was
convinced it would **exalt** the crowd even more than last week's show.

6. _____ Kristen could not tolerate her friend's barking dog any longer and finally
decided to **abhor** her relationship with her neighbors across the street.

7. _____ Phoebe decided as soon as she woke up that she simply would not
tolerate the **tedium** of one more lonely day in this deserted mountain town.

8. _____ If Monica and Jennifer were ever to endure this **nuance** they would
have to find better ways to communicate.

9. _____ Even though Grace was sure she should have won the student council
election, she was too afraid to ask her teacher for a **recant**.

10. _____ It's been more than 100 years since Uncle Andrew's family was forced to
emulate from the distant, cold land his grandfather called the old country.

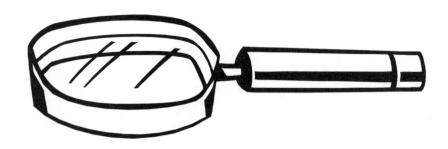

Name: _____

Identify the part of speech for each word and then use each word in an original sentence. Remember that words often can be used as more than one part of speech; if you identify a word as one part of speech, you must use it as that part of speech in your sentence.

Word	Part of Speech	Your Sentence
1. abhor	_____	_____
2. covert	_____	_____
3. emulate	_____	_____
4. exalt	_____	_____
5. hardy	_____	_____
6. leeway	_____	_____
7. nuance	_____	_____
8. recant	_____	_____
9. sustain	_____	_____
10. tedium	_____	_____

◆ **Bonus Work**

Pick three of the vocabulary words above that can be used as more than one part of speech and use each one to write an additional sentence that shows the word being used as a different part of speech than what you used above. You may have to slightly change the form of the word to do this.

Name: _____

abhor   covert   emulate   exalt   hardy
leeway   nuance   recant   sustain   tedium

Below are antonyms for the 10 vocabulary words listed above. Next to each word in the first column, write a vocabulary word that has the opposite meaning. Then, provide a synonym (a word or phrase) in the last column for each vocabulary word.

Antonym	Vocabulary Word	Synonym
condemn	_____	_____
tender	_____	_____
discontinue	_____	_____
admire	_____	_____
restriction	_____	_____
excitement	_____	_____
be a leader	_____	_____
confirm	_____	_____
unconcealed	_____	_____
great variation	_____	_____

Name: _____

Part A—Complete the Ladder

Below are ladders for each of this week's vocabulary words. Two consecutive letters from each word are given. Fill in the missing letters to correctly spell each of the vocabulary words.

1. | | | | l | a | | |

2. | | | | e | r | |

3. | | | | a | n | |

4. | | | a | n | | |

5. | | | e | w | | |

6. | | e | d | | | |

7. | | | a | l | |

8. | | | h | o | |

9. | | a | r | | |

10. | | | | | a | i | |

Name: _____

Part B–Show Your Understanding

Listed below are antonyms for five vocabulary words and synonyms for five vocabulary words. Identify which vocabulary word is related to the antonym or synonym and write it next to the word.

Antonym	Vocabulary Word
1. weak	_____
2. restriction	_____
3. destroy	_____
4. excitement	_____
5. adore	_____

Synonym	Vocabulary Word
6. take back	_____
7. praise	_____
8. hidden	_____
9. imitate	_____
10. slight variation	_____

Unit 8

Name: _____

The 10 mystery words listed below contain this week's vocabulary words. The letters of each vocabulary word appear in the correct order among the letters in the mystery word; however, extra letters have been added to camouflage the vocabulary word. The extra letters can appear before, in between, and after the correct letters. When the mystery word is placed correctly in the grid, the letters of the vocabulary word will appear in the open boxes and the word will be revealed. Write the correct vocabulary word to the right of the grid. You may use a dictionary to complete this exercise.

Example: sladidernings

| | s | l | a | d | i | d | e | r | n | i | n | g | s | = ladder |

1. chursouripe

2. imbipelaine

3. reapipoertie

4. steamiendal

5. swariatoshut

6. tapleancired

7. nestheirenter

8. pipetaruneasty

Name: _____

9. ladiespoleite

10. amioriostein

Finding Meaning

Once you have deciphered all the vocabulary words, use a dictionary to help you learn their meanings. Write each word next to its correct definition.

1. _____ miserable or depressed

2. _____ shine, luster

3. _____ deeply sincere or serious

4. _____ peaceful, quiet

5. _____ a connection or relationship

6. _____ to use up or lessen

7. _____ to take over by force

8. _____ to improve or change to make better

9. _____ anger or rage

10. _____ to show something as false

Name: _____

Determine whether the definition for the vocabulary word is correct. Write true or false on the line before each word.

1. _____ **sheen**—to be smart or quick-witted

2. _____ **wrath**—a spirit or phantom

3. _____ **belie**—to put down or criticize

4. _____ **rapport**—a close, agreeable relationship

5. _____ **deplete**—to banish or export

6. _____ **earnest**—serious or sincere

7. _____ **amend**—to revise or modify

8. _____ **usurp**—to use up or waste

9. _____ **placid**—calm and quiet

10. _____ **morose**—earthly or worldly

Choose three words that you indicated had incorrect definitions and write their correct definitions.

Vocabulary Word   **Definition**

_____   _____

_____   _____

_____   _____

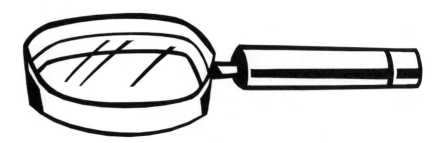

8.3 Parts of Speech

Name: _____

Identify the part of speech for each word and then use each word in an original sentence. Remember that words often can be used as more than one part of speech; if you identify a word as one part of speech, you must use it as that part of speech in your sentence.

Word	Part of Speech	Your Sentence
1. amend	_____	_____
2. belie	_____	_____
3. deplete	_____	_____
4. earnest	_____	_____
5. morose	_____	_____
6. placid	_____	_____
7. rapport	_____	_____
8. sheen	_____	_____
9. usurp	_____	_____
10. wrath	_____	_____

◆ **Bonus Work**
   Pick three of the vocabulary words above that can be used as more than one part of speech and use each one to write an additional sentence that shows the word being used as a different part of speech than what you used above. You may have to slightly change the form of the word to do this.

Name: _____

amend	belie	deplete	earnest	morose
placid	rapport	sheen	usurp	wrath

Below are antonyms for the 10 vocabulary words listed above. Next to each word in the first column, write a vocabulary word that has the opposite meaning. Then, provide a synonym (a word or phrase) in the last column for each vocabulary word.

Antonym	Vocabulary Word	Synonym
replenish	_____	_____
surrender	_____	_____
insincere	_____	_____
keep the same	_____	_____
turbulent	_____	_____
kindness	_____	_____
unfriendliness	_____	_____
prove	_____	_____
dullness	_____	_____
cheerful	_____	_____

Name: _____

Part A–Complete the Ladder

Below are ladders for each of this week's vocabulary words. Two consecutive letters from each word are given. Fill in the missing letters to correctly spell each of the vocabulary words.

1. | | | a | t | |

2. | | | | o | s | |

3. | | | | i | e |

4. | | | e | n | |

5. | | | | l | e | | |

6. | | l | a | | | |

7. | | h | e | | |

8. | | | r | n | | | |

9. | | | u | r | |

10. | | | | | o | r | |

Name: _____

Part B–Show Your Understanding
Write each vocabulary word and provide a short definition.

Vocabulary Word	Definition

1. _____   _____

_____

2. _____   _____

_____

3. _____   _____

_____

4. _____   _____

_____

5. _____   _____

_____

6. _____   _____

_____

7. _____   _____

_____

8. _____   _____

_____

9. _____   _____

_____

10. _____   _____

_____

Name: _____

The 10 mystery words listed below contain this week's vocabulary words. The letters of each vocabulary word appear in the correct order among the letters in the mystery word; however, extra letters have been added to camouflage the vocabulary word. The extra letters can appear before, in between, and after the correct letters. When the mystery word is placed correctly in the grid, the letters of the vocabulary word will appear in the open boxes and the word will be revealed. Write the correct vocabulary word to the right of the grid. You may use a dictionary to complete this exercise.

Example: sladidernings

| | s | l | a | d | i | d | e | r | n | i | n | g | s | = ladder |

1. chealiliowas

2. pealickitint

3. stoutesutter

4. supriofunser

5. tableianesty

6. riverintroll

7. gackleinings

8. densichoirines

Name: _____

9. escouncilseats

□□□□□□□□□□

10. barmemainters

□□□□□□□□□□

Finding Meaning

Once you have deciphered all the vocabulary words, use a dictionary to help you learn their meanings. Write each word next to its correct definition.

1. _____ to reject or refuse

2. _____ to force out

3. _____ preconceived notion

4. _____ to send or pay

5. _____ to draw out or bring out

6. _____ to make sacred or holy

7. _____ similar or compatible

8. _____ to belittle or sneer at

9. _____ plentiful, abundant

10. _____ brief, to the point

Name: _____

Determine whether the vocabulary word in boldface is used correctly. Write
true or false on the line before each sentence.

1. _____ Oliver didn't care if others might **scorn** him; he was excited about
joining the town's Unusual Pets Club.

2. _____ Kyle wasn't able to spend much time working on his scrapbook, so
many of the pages were crooked and **akin**, with pictures sticking out all over
the place.

3. _____ Harris prided himself on being very **concise** when completing work for
school and always put in extra effort elaborating and adding more details than
his teacher asked for.

4. _____ Ned was very pleased with the plan he came up with for helping his
community and hoped everyone in student council would **veto** the idea.

5. _____ His sister believed every word their new neighbors said, but Karl would
only **hallow** their remarks with a disinterested shrug.

6. _____ "Everyone has a **bias**," remarked Judy, "so make sure you only encourage
those who agree with us to come to Thursday's meeting."

7. _____ Denzel tried to **oust** the deer from the backyard without injuring the animal or
his garden.

8. _____ Pearl could not **remit** hearing her grandmother tell all those exciting
stories of her childhood days growing up in Africa.

9. _____ Jose's teacher encouraged everyone to **elicit** their final draft of their
haiku on Friday so they could be graded over the weekend.

10. _____ Meri's aunt owned an oil well that produced a **profuse** river of rich,
dark oil, assuring her an adequate income for years to come.

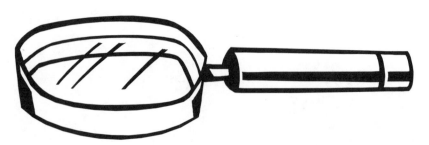

Name: _____

Identify the part of speech for each word and then use each word in an original sentence. Remember that words often can be used as more than one part of speech; if you identify a word as one part of speech, you must use it as that part of speech in your sentence.

Word	Part of Speech	Your Sentence
1. akin	_____	_____
2. bias	_____	_____
3. concise	_____	_____
4. elicit	_____	_____
5. hallow	_____	_____
6. oust	_____	_____
7. profuse	_____	_____
8. remit	_____	_____
9. scorn	_____	_____
10. veto	_____	_____

◆ **Bonus Work**

Pick three of the vocabulary words above that can be used as more than one part of speech and use each one to write an additional sentence that shows the word being used as a different part of speech than what you used above. You may have to slightly change the form of the word to do this.

Name: _____

akin	bias	concise	elicit	hallow
oust	profuse	remit	scorn	veto

Below are antonyms for the 10 vocabulary words listed above. Next to each word in the first column, write a vocabulary word that has the opposite meaning. Then, provide a synonym (a word or phrase) in the last column for each vocabulary word.

Antonym	Vocabulary Word	Synonym
withhold	_____	_____
lengthy	_____	_____
admiration	_____	_____
different	_____	_____
approve	_____	_____
fairness	_____	_____
meager	_____	_____
welcome	_____	_____
suppress	_____	_____
dishonor	_____	_____

Name: _____

Part A–Complete the Ladder

Below are ladders for each of this week's vocabulary words. Two consecutive letters from each word are given. Fill in the missing letters to correctly spell each of the vocabulary words.

1. | | | | | u | s | |

2. | | | i | c | | |

3. | | | | c | i | | |

4. | | e | t | |

5. | | | | l | o | |

6. | | u | s | |

7. | | i | a | |

8. | | | o | r | |

9. | | e | m | | |

10. | | | i | n | |

Name: _____

Part B—Show Your Understanding

Write each vocabulary word on the line next to its closest definition.

1. _____ to remove or kick out

2. _____ to prohibit or forbid

3. _____ to bring out or call forth

4. _____ related, similar, compatible

5. _____ to give payment

6. _____ to make sacred, respect greatly

7. _____ bountiful or abundant

8. _____ personal judgment or preference, often unreasonable

9. _____ to reject or treat as unworthy

10. _____ using few words

Unit 10

Name: _____

The 10 mystery words listed below contain this week's vocabulary words. The letters of each vocabulary word appear in the correct order among the letters in the mystery word; however, extra letters have been added to camouflage the vocabulary word. The extra letters can appear before, in between, and after the correct letters. When the mystery word is placed correctly in the grid, the letters of the vocabulary word will appear in the open boxes and the word will be revealed. Write the correct vocabulary word to the right of the grid. You may use a dictionary to complete this exercise.

Example: sladidernings

	s	l	a	d	i	d	e	r	n	i	n	g	s	= ladder

1. anivetristyne

2. pasikiromistha

3. encreanvitert

4. saganorisithe

5. cabylitzhens

6. spanbiscurding

7. fifliatunoter

8. slylybaricsic

Name: _____

9. grobischurner

☐☐☐☐☐☐☐☐☐☐☐

10. strepiroteach

☐☐☐☐☐☐☐☐☐☐☐

Finding Meaning

Once you have deciphered all the vocabulary words, use a dictionary to help you learn their meanings. Write each word next to its correct definition.

1. _____ carefree and happy

2. _____ bright and showy

3. _____ to express with wild enthusiasm

4. _____ a minor battle or argument

5. _____ to show off or exhibit shamelessly

6. _____ to express criticism or disapproval

7. _____ hidden or out of sight

8. _____ truth, actuality

9. _____ ridiculous or unreasonable

10. _____ pleasant sounding, expressing feelings

Name: _____

Determine whether the definition for the vocabulary word is correct. Write true or false on the line before each word.

1. _____ **blithe**—bent or flexed easily

2. _____ **flaunt**—to find fault with

3. _____ **verity**—truth or reality

4. _____ **skirmish**—to avoid or go round

5. _____ **reproach**—to return or come back

6. _____ **rave**—talk wildly or express great praise

7. _____ **obscure**—submissive

8. _____ **absurd**—enormous, overly large

9. _____ **garish**—tastelessly ornate or showy

10. _____ **lyric**—smooth, song-like, full of emotion

Choose three words that you indicated had incorrect definitions and write their correct definitions.

Vocabulary Word　　　**Definition**

_____　　_____

_____　　_____

_____　　_____

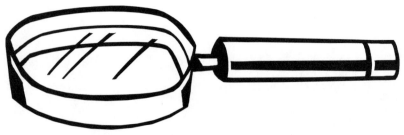

Name: _____

Identify the part of speech for each word and then use each word in an original sentence. Remember that words often can be used as more than one part of speech; if you identify a word as one part of speech, you must use it as that part of speech in your sentence.

Word	Part of Speech	Your Sentence
1. absurd	_____	_____
2. blithe	_____	_____
3. flaunt	_____	_____
4. garish	_____	_____
5. lyric	_____	_____
6. obscure	_____	_____
7. rave	_____	_____
8. reproach	_____	_____
9. skirmish	_____	_____
10. verity	_____	_____

◆ **Bonus Work**

Pick three of the vocabulary words above that can be used as more than one part of speech and use each one to write an additional sentence that shows the word being used as a different part of speech than what you used above. You may have to slightly change the form of the word to do this.

Name: _____

absurd   blithe   flaunt   garish   lyric

obscure   rave   reproach   skirmish   verity

Below are antonyms for the 10 vocabulary words listed above. Next to each word in the first column, write a vocabulary word that has the opposite meaning. Then, provide a synonym (a word or phrase) in the last column for each vocabulary word.

Antonym	Vocabulary Word	Synonym
truce	_____	_____
hide	_____	_____
not poetic	_____	_____
inaccuracy	_____	_____
logical	_____	_____
keep quiet	_____	_____
sorrowful	_____	_____
compliment	_____	_____
clear	_____	_____
drab	_____	_____

Name: _____

Part A Complete the Ladder

Below are ladders for each of this week's vocabulary words. Two consecutive letters from each word are given. Fill in the missing letters to correctly spell each of the vocabulary words.

1. | | | i | t | | |

2. | | a | v | |

3. | | | i | r | | | | |

4. | | | r | i | | |

5. | | | | i | s | |

6. | | | | r | o | | | |

7. | | | | u | r | |

8. | | | | | u | r | |

9. | | | | u | n | |

10. | | | r | i | |

Name: _____

Part B–Show Your Understanding

Use each of the words correctly in an original sentence.

1. _____

   _____

2. _____

   _____

3. _____

   _____

4. _____

   _____

5. _____

   _____

6. _____

   _____

7. _____

   _____

8. _____

   _____

9. _____

   _____

10. _____

    _____

Unit 11

Name: _____

The 10 mystery words listed below contain this week's vocabulary words. The letters of each vocabulary word appear in the correct order among the letters in the mystery word; however, extra letters have been added to camouflage the vocabulary word. The extra letters can appear before, in between, and after the correct letters. When the mystery word is placed correctly in the grid, the letters of the vocabulary word will appear in the open boxes and the word will be revealed. Write the correct vocabulary word to the right of the grid. You may use a dictionary to complete this exercise.

Example: sladidernings

| | s | l | a | d | i | d | e | r | n | i | n | g | s | = ladder |

1. schoondornest

2. irripepriestser

3. paslucecrumobly

4. efferungealine

5. baberatzennels

6. aliarussthernes

7. wespilancraters

8. gaperuxdernents

Name: _____

9. rivteritentexer

10. rhinetrainguess

Finding Meaning

Once you have deciphered all the vocabulary words, use a dictionary to help you learn their meanings. Write each word next to its correct definition.

1. _____ calm down or pacify

2. _____ to arouse interest because of unique or secret features

3. _____ to give in or surrender

4. _____ thrifty or stingy

5. _____ serious or plain

6. _____ careful, sensible

7. _____ bold and shameless

8. _____ highest point, pinnacle

9. _____ accept or allow

10. _____ keep inside or hold back

Name: _____

Determine whether the vocabulary word in boldface is used correctly. Write
true or false on the line before each sentence.

1. _____ We must boldly **succumb** to the idea that some people are better than others if
we are ever to live in a world of peace and compassion.

2. _____ James was often **brazen** and defiant, and he thought nothing of bullying
smaller children right in front of the teachers.

3. _____ Annie's mother often told her to stop being so stiff and **prudent** if she
expected anyone to notice what a great performer she was.

4. _____ Seventh grade was the **vertex** of Cassie's dancing ability, and from
then on her sudden growth spurt made it difficult for her to move her limbs
gracefully.

5. _____ "Don't **repress** your feelings," Miss Crocker would tell her class when
writing poetry. "You should share them freely with the world."

6. _____ Jeremy's behavior seemed to **intrigue** Mama, and she couldn't help but watch
every move he made when they were in the same room.

7. _____ Jack was really looking forward to celebrating the **austere** occasion of his
favorite uncle's promotion with his family next weekend in New York City.

8. _____ Mr. Merton's job was to keep the crowd going, so every time their
cheers died down he would **placate** them with a rousing song on his trumpet.

9. _____ Karen's mother always complained that she was too **frugal**, spending
too much money on wild and unnecessary things.

10. _____ The awards ceremony would be held on Thursday, and Alex couldn't
wait to stand on stage and listen to the principal **condone** his achievement to
the entire school.

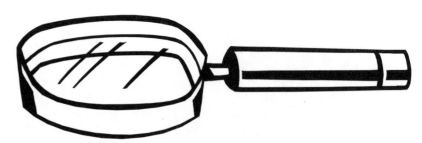

Name: _____

Identify the part of speech for each word and then use each word in an original sentence. Remember that words often can be used as more than one part of speech; if you identify a word as one part of speech, you must use it as that part of speech in your sentence.

Word	Part of Speech	Your Sentence
1. austere	_____	_____
2. brazen	_____	_____
3. condone	_____	_____
4. frugal	_____	_____
5. intrigue	_____	_____
6. placate	_____	_____
7. prudent	_____	_____
8. repress	_____	_____
9. succumb	_____	_____
10. vertex	_____	_____

◆ **Bonus Work**

Pick three of the vocabulary words above that can be used as more than one part of speech and use each one to write an additional sentence that shows the word being used as a different part of speech than what you used above. You may have to slightly change the form of the word to do this.

Name: _____

| austere | brazen | condone | frugal | intrigue |
| placate | prudent | repress | succumb | vertex |

Below are antonyms for the 10 vocabulary words listed above. Next to each word in the first column, write a vocabulary word that has the opposite meaning. Then, provide a synonym (a word or phrase) in the last column for each vocabulary word.

Antonym	Vocabulary Word	Synonym
provoke	_____	_____
resist	_____	_____
wasteful	_____	_____
meek	_____	_____
careless	_____	_____
bore	_____	_____
bottom	_____	_____
let go	_____	_____
adorned	_____	_____
forbid	_____	_____

Name: _____

Part A–Complete the Ladder

Below are ladders for each of this week's vocabulary words. Two consecutive letters from each word are given. Fill in the missing letters to correctly spell each of the vocabulary words.

1. | | | | r | i | | |

2. | | | | t | e | | |

3. | | | a | c | | | |

4. | | r | a | | | |

5. | | r | u | | | |

6. | | | n | d | | | |

7. | | | | t | e | |

8. | | | | r | e | | |

9. | | | | c | u | |

10. | | | | d | e | | |

Name: _____

Part B–Show Your Understanding

Listed below are antonyms for five vocabulary words and synonyms for five vocabulary words. Identify which vocabulary word is related to the antonym or synonym and write it next to the word.

Antonym	Vocabulary Word
1. enrage	_____
2. disapprove	_____
3. base	_____
4. discreet	_____
5. reckless	_____

Synonym	Vocabulary Word
6. fascinate	_____
7. thrifty	_____
8. surrender	_____
9. serious	_____
10. inhibit	_____

Unit 12

Name: _____

The 10 mystery words listed below contain this week's vocabulary words. The letters of each vocabulary word appear in the correct order among the letters in the mystery word; however, extra letters have been added to camouflage the vocabulary word. The extra letters can appear before, in between, and after the correct letters. When the mystery word is placed correctly in the grid, the letters of the vocabulary word will appear in the open boxes and the word will be revealed. Write the correct vocabulary word to the right of the grid. You may use a dictionary to complete this exercise.

Example: sladidernings

| | s | l | a | d | i | d | e | r | n | i | n | g | s | = ladder |

1. gagaguachaires

2. sapriolinfixic

3. ghasitruthsens

4. eldrilingernot

5. bestearinkers

6. pasithorileakin

7. accusurtstorys

8. trunkrouslyst

Name: _____

9. prinsecinteller

10. maidencityswivels

Finding Meaning

Once you have deciphered all the vocabulary words, use a dictionary to help you learn their meanings. Write each word next to its correct definition.

1. _____ certain or clear-thinking

2. _____ vulgar or tacky

3. _____ to provoke or stir up

4. _____ productive or abundant

5. _____ disobedient or wild

6. _____ smart or perceptive

7. _____ superficial, hasty

8. _____ careful or hard-working

9. _____ screech

10. _____ barren or unadorned

Name: _____

Determine whether the definition for the vocabulary word is correct. Write true or false on the line before each word.

1. _____ **decisive**—creating disagreement or separation

2. _____ **prolific**—having romantic imagery

3. _____ **incite**—to provoke or cause to happen

4. _____ **gauche**—to cut or scoop out

5. _____ **unruly**—ungovernable

6. _____ **cursory**—filled with evil or misfortune

7. _____ **astute**—showing superior powers of the intellect

8. _____ **shriek**—a shrill, frantic outburst

9. _____ **diligent**—showing superficial interest

10. _____ **stark**—frighten or surprise suddenly

Choose three words that you indicated had incorrect definitions and write their correct definitions.

Vocabulary Word   **Definition**

_____   _____

_____   _____

_____   _____

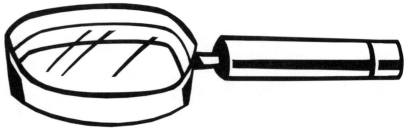

12.3 Parts of Speech

Name: _____

Identify the part of speech for each word and then use each word in an original sentence. Remember that words often can be used as more than one part of speech; if you identify a word as one part of speech, you must use it as that part of speech in your sentence.

Word	Part of Speech	Your Sentence
1. astute	_____	_____
2. cursory	_____	_____
3. decisive	_____	_____
4. diligent	_____	_____
5. gauche	_____	_____
6. incite	_____	_____
7. prolific	_____	_____
8. shriek	_____	_____
9. stark	_____	_____
10. unruly	_____	_____

◆ **Bonus Work**

Pick three of the vocabulary words above that can be used as more than one part of speech and use each one to write an additional sentence that shows the word being used as a different part of speech than what you used above. You may have to slightly change the form of the word to do this.

Name: _____

astute	cursory	decisive	diligent	gauche
incite	prolific	shriek	stark	unruly

Below are antonyms for the 10 vocabulary words listed above. Next to each word in the first column, write a vocabulary word that has the opposite meaning. Then, provide a synonym (a word or phrase) in the last column for each vocabulary word.

Antonym	Vocabulary Word	Synonym
ornate	_____	_____
lazy	_____	_____
murmur	_____	_____
naïve	_____	_____
thorough	_____	_____
obedient	_____	_____
tasteful	_____	_____
discourage	_____	_____
unproductive	_____	_____
uncertain	_____	_____

Name: _____

Part A—Complete the Ladder

Below are ladders for each of this week's vocabulary words. Two consecutive letters from each word are given. Fill in the missing letters to correctly spell each of the vocabulary words.

1. | | | c | i | | |

2. | | | c | i | | | |

3. | | | l | i | | | |

4. | | | r | u | | |

5. | | | a | r | |

6. | | | t | u | | |

7. | | | r | i | | |

8. | | | u | c | | |

9. | | | o | l | | | |

10. | | | | s | o | |

Name: _____

Part B—Show Your Understanding

Write each word and provide a short definition.

Vocabulary Word	**Definition**

1. _____   _____

   _____

2. _____   _____

   _____

3. _____   _____

   _____

4. _____   _____

   _____

5. _____   _____

   _____

6. _____   _____

   _____

7. _____   _____

   _____

8. _____   _____

   _____

9. _____   _____

   _____

10. _____   _____

   _____

Unit 13

Name: _____

The 10 mystery words listed below contain this week's vocabulary words. The letters of each vocabulary word appear in the correct order among the letters in the mystery word; however, extra letters have been added to camouflage the vocabulary word. The extra letters can appear before, in between, and after the correct letters. When the mystery word is placed correctly in the grid, the letters of the vocabulary word will appear in the open boxes and the word will be revealed. Write the correct vocabulary word to the right of the grid. You may use a dictionary to complete this exercise.

Example: sladidernings

| | s | l | a | d | i | d | e | r | n | i | n | g | s | = ladder |

1. eglixblerantest

2. staffordgotten

3. plesourepanses

4. trexapredaiters

5. irrespollutrents

6. scorntrailteller

7. applagliaraized

8. pippencathanites

Name: _____

9. cyclopsinourset

10. gravitasidolly

Finding Meaning

Once you have deciphered all the vocabulary words, use a dictionary to help you learn their meanings. Write each word next to its correct definition.

1. _____ to go beyond or exceed

2. _____ to build, form, or invent; to move ahead

3. _____ showing firmness and determination

4. _____ to speed up the process of

5. _____ having a strong preference or liking

6. _____ large in number or quantity

7. _____ to present someone else's words or thoughts as your own

8. _____ feeling regret or remorse; affected by guilt

9. _____ enthusiastic or keenly interested in something

10. _____ to release, give equal rights to

Name: _____

Determine whether the vocabulary word in boldface is used correctly. Write true or false on the line before each sentence.

1. _____ "It's like trying to get blood from a stone," thought Shelby, as she tried to fetch another cup of water from the **copious** supply in the dried-out well.

2. _____ Harry was sure that with a little practice and a little hard work he could **surpass** even his mother's great success.

3. _____ Ginny's father loved adventure and couldn't wait to take the family on an Egyptian adventure and **expedite** through the pyramids.

4. _____ Jenny was very **resolute** about doing whatever her classmates wanted and whined and complained every time they asked for a favor.

5. _____ Tyler often told them that they could only **liberate** themselves from their deepest, darkest fears when they followed the highest calling of their own hearts.

6. _____ Neville knew he shouldn't **plagiarize** other people's work, but he didn't care as long as he didn't get caught and he could get a good grade for the work.

7. _____ Ron had a very **avid** reaction to his friend's frightening plans to wander through the deserted village without any means of protection.

8. _____ Presley had a **penchant** for peacefulness and could always be counted on to avoid fighting by simply walking away from a confrontation.

9. _____ "If you were truly **contrite**," said Molly, "you wouldn't smirk or giggle when making an apology."

10. _____ "Please don't **forge** the lock," cried Violet. "If it doesn't open easily I'd rather find another way to get in."

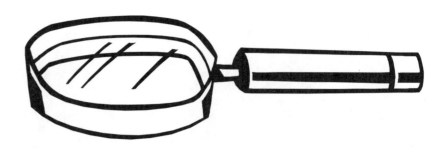

13.3 Parts of Speech

Name: _____

Identify the part of speech for each word and then use each word in an original sentence. Remember that words often can be used as more than one part of speech; if you identify a word as one part of speech, you must use it as that part of speech in your sentence.

Word	Part of Speech	Your Sentence
1. avid	_____	_____
2. contrite	_____	_____
3. copious	_____	_____
4. expedite	_____	_____
5. forge	_____	_____
6. liberate	_____	_____
7. penchant	_____	_____
8. plagiarize	_____	_____
9. resolute	_____	_____
10. surpass	_____	_____

◆ **Bonus Work**

Pick three of the vocabulary words above that can be used as more than one part of speech and use each one to write an additional sentence that shows the word being used as a different part of speech than what you used above. You may have to slightly change the form of the word to do this.

Name: _____

| avid | contrite | copious | expedite | forge |
| liberate | penchant | plagiarize | resolute | surpass |

Below are antonyms for the 10 vocabulary words listed above. Next to each word in the first column, write a vocabulary word that has the opposite meaning. Then, provide a synonym (a word or phrase) in the last column for each vocabulary word.

Antonym	Vocabulary Word	Synonym
originate	_____	_____
scarce	_____	_____
indifferent	_____	_____
lag behind	_____	_____
undetermined	_____	_____
unremorseful	_____	_____
aversion	_____	_____
demolish	_____	_____
enslave	_____	_____
slow down	_____	_____

Name: _____

Part A—Complete the Ladder

Below are ladders for each of this week's vocabulary words. Two consecutive letters from each word are given. Fill in the missing letters to correctly spell each of the vocabulary words.

1. | | | p | e | | | |

2. | | | p | i | | |

3. | | | | | h | a | | |

4. | | v | i | |

5. | | | n | t | | | |

6. | | o | r | | |

7. | | | r | p | | |

8. | | | | e | r | | |

9. | | | s | o | | | |

10. | | | | | i | a | | | | |

Name: _____

Part B–Show Your Understanding

Write each vocabulary word on the line next to its closest definition.

1. _____ to build or create

2. _____ remorseful, repentant

3. _____ liking or fondness

4. _____ enthusiastic or eager

5. _____ to release

6. _____ abundant or plentiful

7. _____ to exceed or outdo

8. _____ to speed up or hasten

9. _____ to copy illegally

10. _____ determined or firm

Unit 14

Name: _____

The 10 mystery words listed below contain this week's vocabulary words. The letters of each vocabulary word appear in the correct order among the letters in the mystery word; however, extra letters have been added to camouflage the vocabulary word. The extra letters can appear before, in between, and after the correct letters. When the mystery word is placed correctly in the grid, the letters of the vocabulary word will appear in the open boxes and the word will be revealed. Write the correct vocabulary word to the right of the grid. You may use a dictionary to complete this exercise.

Example: sladidernings

	s	l	a	d	i	d	e	r	n	i	n

g s   = ladder

1. pajelosparndeys

2. rainfruprigates

3. smeddelsuddems

4. presidionauntry

5. michonytreatry

6. tomertcutrinally

7. experitionrents

8. farmingwarblers

Name: _____

9. ebayboyscoutty

10. bestegareglaten

Finding Meaning

Once you have deciphered all the vocabulary words, use a dictionary to help you learn their meanings. Write each word next to its correct definition.

1. _____ to deceive or mislead

2. _____ danger or risk

3. _____ quick and changeable

4. _____ friendly, agreeable

5. _____ to separate or keep apart

6. _____ booming, echoing, or resounding

7. _____ related or important

8. _____ reject or refuse

9. _____ different or opposing

10. _____ to enrage or annoy

Name: _____

Determine whether the definition for the vocabulary word is correct. Write true or false on the line before each word.

1. _____ **jeopardy**—protectiveness

2. _____ **delude**—gobble up

3. _____ **segregate**—isolate

4. _____ **boycott**—reject

5. _____ **infuriate**—damage

6. _____ **pertinent**—valuable

7. _____ **contrary**—conflicting

8. _____ **resonant**—opposed to

9. _____ **amiable**—good-humored

10. _____ **mercurial**—compassionate

Choose three words that you indicated had incorrect definitions and write their correct definitions.

Vocabulary Word   **Definition**

_____   _____

_____   _____

_____   _____

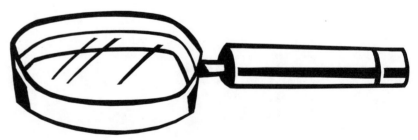

14.3 Parts of Speech

Name: _____

Identify the part of speech for each word and then use each word in an original sentence. Remember that words often can be used as more than one part of speech; if you identify a word as one part of speech, you must use it as that part of speech in your sentence.

Word	Part of Speech	Your Sentence
1. amiable	_____	_____
2. boycott	_____	_____
3. contrary	_____	_____
4. delude	_____	_____
5. infuriate	_____	_____
6. jeopardy	_____	_____
7. mercurial	_____	_____
8. pertinent	_____	_____
9. resonant	_____	_____
10. segregate	_____	_____

◆ **Bonus Work**
   Pick three of the vocabulary words above that can be used as more than one part of speech and use each one to write an additional sentence that shows the word being used as a different part of speech than what you used above. You may have to slightly change the form of the word to do this.

Name: _____

amiable   boycott   contrary   delude   infuriate
jeopardy   mercurial   pertinent   resonant   segregate

Below are antonyms for the 10 vocabulary words listed above. Next to each word in the first column, write a vocabulary word that has the opposite meaning. Then, provide a synonym (a word or phrase) in the last column for each vocabulary word.

Antonym	Vocabulary Word	Synonym
soothe	_____	_____
irrelevant	_____	_____
support	_____	_____
unvarying	_____	_____
unite	_____	_____
agreeable	_____	_____
antisocial	_____	_____
be truthful	_____	_____
quiet	_____	_____
security	_____	_____

Name: _____

Part A–Complete the Ladder

Below are ladders for each of this week's vocabulary words. Two consecutive letters from each word are given. Fill in the missing letters to correctly spell each of the vocabulary words.

1. | | | | r | e | | | | |

2. | | | | c | o | | |

3. | | | | | a | r | | |

4. | | e | l | | | |

5. | | | | | i | n | | | |

6. | | | | | r | i | | | |

7. | | | | | n | a | | |

8. | | | | | a | r | |

9. | | | | | | r | i | |

10. | | | i | a | | | |

Name: _____

Part B—Show Your Understanding

Use each of the words correctly in an original sentence.

1. _____

   _____

2. _____

   _____

3. _____

   _____

4. _____

   _____

5. _____

   _____

6. _____

   _____

7. _____

   _____

8. _____

   _____

9. _____

   _____

10. _____

   _____

Unit 15

Name: _____

The 10 mystery words listed below contain this week's vocabulary words. The letters of each vocabulary word appear in the correct order among the letters in the mystery word; however, extra letters have been added to camouflage the vocabulary word. The extra letters can appear before, in between, and after the correct letters. When the mystery word is placed correctly in the grid, the letters of the vocabulary word will appear in the open boxes and the word will be revealed. Write the correct vocabulary word to the right of the grid. You may use a dictionary to complete this exercise.

Example: sladidernings

| | s | l | a | d | i | d | e | r | n | i | n | g | s | = ladder |

1. pedestreetread

2. addivilsivatend

3. prexionearapter

4. wisquebiltimeter

5. crabbyscounders

6. tearsevenersell

7. shinstegarcitylad

8. nannanomaulyste

Name: _____

9. equentiverailman

10. annexotophyates

Finding Meaning

Once you have deciphered all the vocabulary words, use a dictionary to help you learn their meanings. Write each word next to its correct definition.

1. _____ to admire or look up to

2. _____ break out or run away

3. _____ amateur or beginner

4. _____ inconsistency or irregularity

5. _____ honesty and uprightness

6. _____ to clear or pardon

7. _____ troublesome; creating disunity

8. _____ awe-inspiring, supreme, or noble

9. _____ to put off or prevent

10. _____ uncover or reveal

Name: _____

Determine whether the vocabulary word in boldface is used correctly. Write true or false on the line before each sentence.

1. _____ Kamalani was the most supportive sister and would do anything to help **deter** her siblings from achieving great success.

2. _____ If Bernadette knew one thing for certain, it was that she alone could not produce enough evidence to **exonerate** herself from the accusations of her enemies.

3. _____ Riley was a **neophyte**; therefore, she was called upon every time someone needed an expert opinion.

4. _____ "I don't think a person has much **integrity** if all they do is lie and cheat," Carmen told her professor.

5. _____ Mrs. Baudelaire felt it was important to expose her children to the more **sublime** aspects of life and often took them to the symphony, museums, and even poetry readings.

6. _____ Klaus seemed to **revere** everything the author wrote and would avoid his books at all costs.

7. _____ It was true that Mr. Banderas always enjoyed fresh juice at home, so having it at the restaurant was just another **anomaly**.

8. _____ "I'm opposed to everything the council does," said Kiki, "and I can't just stand by while you try to **unveil** their selfish actions from the others."

9. _____ Josef was often **divisive**, doing whatever he could to ensure that nothing went smoothly.

10. _____ Aunt Connie did not want to **abscond** the truth, but she just didn't feel comfortable letting the children know the details of her previous life as a firefighter.

Name: _____

Identify the part of speech for each word and then use each word in an original sentence. Remember that words often can be used as more than one part of speech; if you identify a word as one part of speech, you must use it as that part of speech in your sentence.

Word	Part of Speech	Your Sentence
1. abscond	_____	_____
2. anomaly	_____	_____
3. deter	_____	_____
4. divisive	_____	_____
5. exonerate	_____	_____
6. integrity	_____	_____
7. neophyte	_____	_____
8. revere	_____	_____
9. sublime	_____	_____
10. unveil	_____	_____

◆ **Bonus Work**

Pick three of the vocabulary words above that can be used as more than one part of speech and use each one to write an additional sentence that shows the word being used as a different part of speech than what you used above. You may have to slightly change the form of the word to do this.

Name: _____

| abscond | anomaly | deter | divisive | exonerate |
| integrity | neophyte | revere | sublime | unveil |

Below are antonyms for the 10 vocabulary words listed above. Next to each word in the first column, write a vocabulary word that has the opposite meaning. Then, provide a synonym (a word or phrase) in the last column for each vocabulary word.

Antonym	Vocabulary Word	Synonym
conceal	_____	_____
lowly	_____	_____
encourage	_____	_____
expert	_____	_____
dishonesty	_____	_____
condemn	_____	_____
causing agreement	_____	_____
despise	_____	_____
regularity	_____	_____
remain	_____	_____

Name: _____

Part A—Complete the Ladder

Below are ladders for each of this week's vocabulary words. Two consecutive letters from each word are given. Fill in the missing letters to correctly spell each of the vocabulary words.

1. | | | | i | s | | | |

2. | | | v | e | | |

3. | | | e | i | |

4. | | e | t | | |

5. | | | t | e | | | | | |

6. | | | o | p | | | | |

7. | | | | l | i | | |

8. | | | | c | o | | | |

9. | | | o | n | | | | | |

10. | | | o | m | | | |

Name: _____

Part B–Show Your Understanding

Listed below are antonyms for five vocabulary words and synonyms for five vocabulary words. Identify which vocabulary word is related to the antonym or synonym and write it next to the word.

Antonym	Vocabulary Word
1. encourage	_____
2. dishonesty	_____
3. veteran	_____
4. despise	_____
5. cooperative	_____

Synonym	Vocabulary Word
1. expose	_____
2. pardon	_____
3. abnormality	_____
4. escape	_____
5. inspirational	_____

Answer Key

1.1 Unlocking the Mystery

1. albironader = abroad

2. sapendingreen = pedigree

3. malporfitsy = lofty

4. balerfulny = baleful

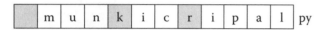

5. munkicripalpy = municipal

6. citharstern = chasten

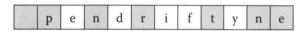

7. pendriftyne = edify

8. spinelpert = inept

9. fersevently = fervent

10. supremiciser = premise

1.1 Finding Meaning

1. edify	2. lofty	3. municipal
4. premise	5. abroad	6. inept
7. chasten	8. pedigree	9. fervent
10. baleful		

1.2 True and False

1. F	2. T	3. F
4. T	5. F	6. T
7. T	8. F	9. T
10. F		

1.3 Parts of Speech

Answers may vary depending on how the student uses the word, but generally the words are identified as the following parts of speech.

1. abroad—adjective
2. baleful—adjective
3. chasten—verb
4. edify—verb
5. fervent—adjective
6. inept—adjective

7. lofty—adjective
8. municipal—adjective
9. pedigree—noun or adjective
10. premise—noun

1.4 Antonyms and Synonyms

Antonym	Word	Synonym
humble	lofty	Answer will vary.
at home	abroad	Answer will vary.
conclusion	premise	Answer will vary.
able	inept	Answer will vary.
harmless	baleful	Answer will vary.
pamper	chasten	Answer will vary.
baffle	edify	Answer will vary.
global	municipal	Answer will vary.
descendants	pedigree	Answer will vary.
indifferent	fervent	Answer will vary.

1.5 Test

Part A

1. baleful	2. abroad	3. pedigree
4. edify	5. chasten	6. lofty
7. inept	8. premise	9. fervent
10. municipal		

Part B

1. inept	2. municipal	3. edify
4. baleful	5. abroad	6. pedigree
7. lofty	8. premise	9. fervent
10. chasten		

2.1 Unlocking the Mystery

1. macorindy = acrid

2. scarndild = candid

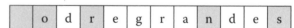

3. odregrandes = degrade

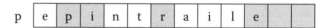

4. pepintraile = entail

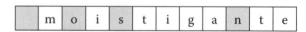

5. loepenireant = lenient

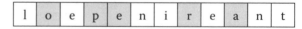

6. moistigante = mitigate

7. suspeaceton = pact

130

2.1 Unlocking the Mystery, continued

8. tarencosils = recoil

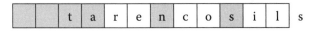

9. askerphtico = skeptic

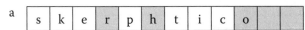

10. civiloifry = vilify

2.1 Finding Meaning
1. lenient
2. skeptic
3. recoil
4. acrid
5. degrade
6. candid
7. mitigate
8. entail
9. pact
10. vilify

2.2 True or False
1. T
2. T
3. F
4. T
5. T
6. F
7. F
8. T
9. F
10. F

2.3 Parts of Speech
Answers may vary depending on how the student uses the word, but generally the words are identified as the following parts of speech.
1. acrid—adjective
2. candid—adjective
3. degrade—verb
4. entail—verb
5. lenient—adjective
6. mitigate—verb
7. pact—noun
8. recoil—verb
9. skeptic—noun
10. vilify—verb

2.4 Antonyms and Synonyms

Antonym	Word	Synonym
compliment	degrade	Answer will vary.
insincere	candid	Answer will vary.
disagreement	pact	Answer will vary.
strict	lenient	Answer will vary.
glorify	vilify	Answer will vary.
believer	skeptic	Answer will vary.
fragrant	acrid	Answer will vary.
intensify	mitigate	Answer will vary.
move toward	recoil	Answer will vary.
not be necessary	entail	Answer will vary.

2.5 Test
Part A
1. degrade
2. pact
3. lenient
4. acrid
5. candid
6. mitigate
7. skeptic
8. vilify
9. recoil
10. entail

Part B
Original sentences will vary.

3.1 Unlocking the Mystery

1. gafoilbiles = foible

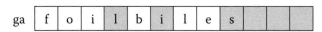

2. tranceutaen = acute

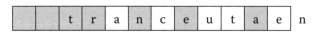

3. modlilifry = mollify

4. strawndrey = tawdry

5. scabajercot = abject

6. famutoilane = futile

7. dielungest = deluge

8. pentvenliop = envelop

9. tresclisuses = recluse

10. shrubatiles = subtle

3.1 Finding Meaning
1. deluge
2. foible
3. tawdry
4. acute
5. envelop
6. recluse
7. subtle
8. mollify
9. futile
10. abject

3.2 True or False
1. T
2. T
3. F
4. T
5. T
6. F
7. F
8. T
9. F
10. F

3.3 Parts of Speech
Answers may vary depending on how the student uses the word, but generally the words are identified as the following parts of speech..
1. abject—adjective
2. acute—adjective
3. deluge—noun or verb
4. envelop—verb
5. foible—noun
6. futile—adjective
7. mollify—verb
8. recluse—noun
9. subtle—adjective
10. tawdry—adjective

Answer Key

3.4 Antonyms and Synonyms

Antonym	Word	Synonym
obvious	subtle	Answer will vary.
moderate	acute	Answer will vary.
tasteful	tawdry	Answer will vary.
productive	futile	Answer will vary.
drought	deluge	Answer will vary.
enrage	mollify	Answer will vary.
strength	foible	Answer will vary.
hopeful	abject	Answer will vary.
socialite	recluse	Answer will vary.
uncover	envelop	Answer will vary.

3.5 Test

Part A

1. mollify
2. futile
3. foible
4. deluge
5. abject
6. recluse
7. acute
8. envelop
9. tawdry
10. subtle

Part B

1. mollify
2. foible
3. abject
4. acute
5. tawdry
6. futile
7. deluge
8. recluse
9. envelop
10. subtle

4.1 Unlocking the Mystery

1. arkisnedliners = kindle

2. egrianunite = gaunt

3. effiorntest = forte

4. arvioglurter = vogue

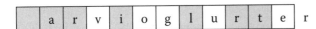

5. pellsundie = elude

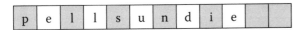

6. semealigion = malign

7. bonivearist = overt

8. eustoalidress = staid

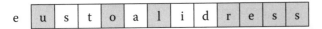

9. pallauchinder = lucid

p	a	l	l	a	u	c	h	i	n	d	e	r

10. crinampedell = impede

	c	r	i	n	a	m	p	e	d	e	ll

4.1 Finding Meaning

1. lucid
2. staid
3. impede
4. elude
5. forte
6. vogue
7. kindle
8. malign
9. gaunt
10. overt

4.2 True or False

1. T
2. T
3. F
4. T
5. T
6. F
7. F
8. F
9. F
10. T

4.3 Parts of Speech

Answers may vary depending on how the student uses the word, but generally the words are identified as the following parts of speech.

1. elude—verb
2. forte—noun
3. gaunt—adjective
4. impede—verb
5. kindle—verb
6. lucid—adjective
7. malign—verb, adjective
8. overt—adjective
9. staid—adjective
10. vogue—noun, adjective

4.4 Antonyms and Synonyms

Antonym	Word	Synonym
confused	lucid	Answer will vary.
unpopularity	vogue	Answer will vary.
plump	gaunt	Answer will vary.
encounter	elude	Answer will vary.
advance	impede	Answer will vary.
weakness	forte	Answer will vary.
extinguish	kindle	Answer will vary.
hidden	overt	Answer will vary.
praise	malign	Answer will vary.
adventurous	staid	Answer will vary.

4.5 Test

Part A

1. overt
2. impede
3. forte
4. elude
5. gaunt
6. malign
7. vogue
8. lucid
9. kindle
10. staid

Part B

Definitions will vary

5.1 Unlocking the Mystery

1. abiolisatera = bolster

2. evearbloste = verbose

3. speersitaloys = peril

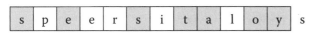

4. pimsingules = mingle

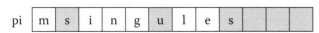

5. meschouffy = scoff

6. vandroiditer = adroit

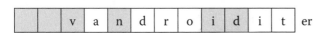

7. sapprosents = prose

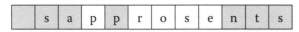

8. stairiflagle = trifle

9. exaplimoist = exploit

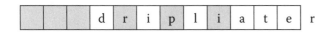

10. dripliater = dilate

5.1 Finding Meaning

1. bolster   2. trifle   3. dilate
4. adroit   5. verbose   6. mingle
7. prose   8. exploit   9. scoff
10. peril

5.2 True or False

1. T   2. T   3. F
4. F   5. F   6. T
7. T   8. F   9. T
10. T

5.3 Parts of Speech

Answers may vary depending on how the student uses the word, but generally the words are identified as the following parts of speech.

1. adroit—adjective   2. bolster—verb, noun
3. dilate—verb   4. exploit—verb, noun
5. mingle—verb   6. peril—noun, verb

7. prose—noun, verb, adjective   8. scoff—verb
9. trifle—noun, verb   10. verbose—adjective

5.4 Antonyms and Synonyms

Antonym	Word	Synonym
shrink	dilate	Answer will vary.
poetry	prose	Answer will vary.
treat fairly	exploit	Answer will vary.
awkward	adroit	Answer will vary.
stay separate	mingle	Answer will vary.
weaken	bolster	Answer will vary.
safety	peril	Answer will vary.
a lot	trifle	Answer will vary.
concise	verbose	Answer will vary.
applaud	scoff	Answer will vary.

5.5 Test

Part A

1. scoff   2. trifle   3. exploit
4. prose   5. bolster   6. adroit
7. peril   8. dilate   9. verbose
10. mingle

Part B

1. verbose   2. peril   3. trifle
4. prose   5. scoff   6. bolster
7. exploit   8. mingle   9. dilate
10. adroit

6.1 Unlocking the Mystery

1. tinniastoes = innate

2. pitherislope = terse

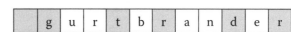

3. gurtbrander = urbane

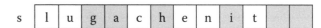

4. slugachenit = lucent

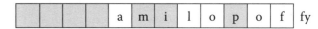

5. amilopoffy = aloof

6. mobatrupsen = obtuse

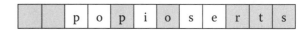

7. popioserts = poise

8. hainadear = hinder

133

9. stumbodule = subdue

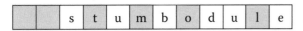

10. leandiorstep = endorse

6.1 Finding Meaning

1. lucent	2. terse	3. hinder
4. subdue	5. obtuse	6. innate
7. urbane	8. poise	9. aloof
10. endorse		

6.2 True or False

1. T	2. F	3. F
4. T	5. F	6. F
7. T	8. F	9. T
10. F		

6.3 Parts of Speech

Answers may vary depending on how the student uses the word, but generally the words are identified as the following part of speech.

1. aloof—adjective	2. endorse—verb
3. hinder—verb	4. innate—adjective
5. lucent—adjective	6. obtuse—adjective
7. poise—noun	8. subdue—verb
9. terse—adjective	10. urbane—adjective

6.4 Antonyms and Synonyms

Antonym	Word	Synonym
long-winded	terse	Answer will vary.
acquired	innate	Answer will vary.
help	hinder	Answer will vary.
disapprove	endorse	Answer will vary.
awkwardness	poise	Answer will vary.
unsophisticated	urbane	Answer will vary.
sharp	obtuse	Answer will vary.
friendly	aloof	Answer will vary.
opaque	lucent	Answer will vary.
release	subdue	Answer will vary.

6.5 Test

Part A

1. aloof	2. terse	3. lucent
4. poise	5. subdue	6. endorse
7. urbane	8. obtuse	9. hinder
10. innate		

Part B

Original sentences will vary.

7.1 Unlocking the Mystery

1. renchainten = recant

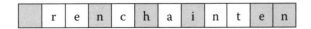

2. sabithorite = abhor

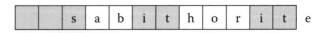

3. pleadeswary = leeway

4. steadisume = tedium

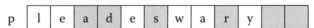

5. choviserate = covert

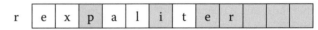

6. rexpaliter = exalt

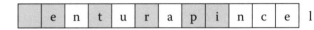

7. enturapincel = nuance

8. thisarudyne = hardy

9. enstustraning = sustain

10. germuslatern = emulate

7.1 Finding Meaning

1. recant	2. emulate	3. abhor
4. tedium	5. exalt	6. nuance
7. leeway	8. hardy	9. covert
10. sustain		

7.2 True or False

1. T	2. T	3. T
4. F	5. F	6. F
7. T	8. F	9. F
10. F		

7.3 Parts of Speech

Answers may vary depending on how the student uses the word, but generally the words are identified as the following parts of speech.

1. abhor—verb	2. covert—adjective
3. emulate—verb	4. exalt—verb
5. hardy—adjective	6. leeway—noun
7. nuance—noun	8. recant—verb
9. sustain—verb	10. tedium—noun

7.4 Antonyms and Synonyms

Antonym	Word	Synonym
condemn	exalt	Answer will vary.
tender	hardy	Answer will vary.
discontinue	sustain	Answer will vary.
admire	abhor	Answer will vary.
restriction	leeway	Answer will vary.
excitement	tedium	Answer will vary.
be a leader	emulate	Answer will vary.
confirm	recant	Answer will vary.
unconcealed	covert	Answer will vary.
great variation	nuance	Answer will vary.

7.5 Test

Part A
1. emulate
2. covert
3. recant
4. nuance
5. leeway
6. tedium
7. exalt
8. abhor
9. hardy
10. sustain

Part B
1. hardy
2. leeway
3. sustain
4. tedium
5. abhor
6. recant
7. exalt
8. covert
9. emulate
10. nuance

8.1 Unlocking the Mystery

1. chursouripe = usurp

ch | u | r | s | o | u | r | i | p | e | | |

2. imbipelaine = belie

| i | m | b | i | p | e | l | a | i | n | e |

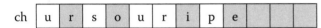

3. reapipoertie = rapport

r | e | a | p | i | p | o | e | r | t | i | e

4. steamiendal = amend

| | s | t | e | a | m | i | e | n | d | a | l

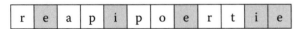

5. swariatoshut = wrath

| | s | w | a | r | i | a | t | o | s | h | ut

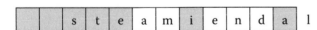

6. tapleancired = placid

t | a | p | l | e | a | n | c | i | r | e | d

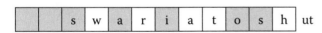

7. nestheirenter = sheen

ne | s | t | h | e | i | r | e | n | t | e | r

8. pipetaruneasty = earnest

p | i | p | e | t | a | r | u | n | e | a | s | t | y

9. ladiespoleite = deplete

la | d | i | e | s | p | o | l | e | i | t | e |

10. amioriostein = morose

| a | m | i | o | r | i | o | s | t | e | i | n |

8.1 Finding Meaning

1. morose
2. sheen
3. earnest
4. placid
5. rapport
6. deplete
7. usurp
8. amend
9. wrath
10. belie

8.2 True or False

1. F
2. F
3. F
4. T
5. F
6. T
7. T
8. F
9. T
10. F

8.3 Parts of Speech

Answers may vary depending on how the student uses the word, but generally the words are identified as the following parts of speech.

1. amend—verb
2. belie—verb
3. deplete—verb
4. earnest—adjective
5. morose—adjective
6. placid—adjective
7. rapport—noun
8. sheen—noun
9. usurp—verb
10. wrath—noun

8.4 Antonyms and Synonyms

Antonym	Word	Synonym
replenish	deplete	Answer will vary.
surrender	usurp	Answer will vary.
insincere	earnest	Answer will vary.
keep the same	amend	Answer will vary.
turbulent	placid	Answer will vary.
kindness	wrath	Answer will vary.
unfriendliness	rapport	Answer will vary.
prove	belie	Answer will vary.
dullness	sheen	Answer will vary.
cheerful	morose	Answer will vary.

8.5 Test

Part A
1. wrath
2. morose
3. belie
4. amend
5. deplete
6. placid
7. sheen
8. earnest
9. usurp
10. rapport

Part B
Definitions will vary.

9.1 Unlocking the Mystery

1. chealiliowas = hallow

2. pealickitint = elicit

3. stoutesutter = oust

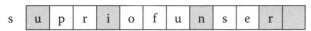

4. supriofunser = profuse

5. tableianesty = bias

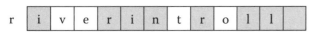

6. riverintroll = veto

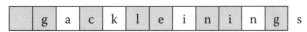

7. gackleinings = akin

8. densichoirines = scorn

9. escouncilseats = concise

10. barmemainters = remit

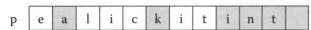

9.1 Finding Meaning

1. veto
2. oust
3. bias
4. remit
5. elicit
6. hallow
7. akin
8. scorn
9. profuse
10. concise

9.2 True or False

1. T
2. F
3. F
4. F
5. F
6. T
7. T
8. F
9. F
10. T

9.3 Parts of Speech

Answers may vary depending on how the student uses the word, but the words are generally identified as the following parts of speech.

1. akin—adjective
2. bias—noun
3. concise—adjective
4. elicit—verb
5. hallow—verb
6. oust—verb
7. profuse—adjective
8. remit—verb
9. scorn—noun, verb
10. veto—verb

9.4 Antonyms and Synonyms

Antonym	Word	Synonym
withhold	remit	Answer will vary.
lengthy	concise	Answer will vary.
admiration	scorn	Answer will vary.
different	akin	Answer will vary.
approve	veto	Answer will vary.
open mindedness	bias	Answer will vary.
meager	profuse	Answer will vary.
welcome	oust	Answer will vary.
suppress	elicit	Answer will vary.
dishonor	hallow	Answer will vary.

9.5 Test

Part A

1. profuse
2. elicit
3. concise
4. veto
5. hallow
6. oust
7. bias
8. scorn
9. remit
10. akin

Part B

1. oust
2. veto
3. elicit
4. akin
5. remit
6. hallow
7. profuse
8. bias
9. scorn
10. concise

10.1 Unlocking the Mystery

1. anivetritsyne = verity

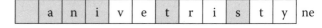

2. pasikiromistha = skirmish

3. ecreanvitert = rave

4. saganorisithe = garish

5. cabylitzhens = blithe

6. spanbiscurding = absurd

7. fifliatunoter = flaunt

10.1 Unlocking the Mystery, continued

8. slylybaricsic = lyric

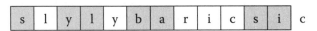

9. grobischurner = obscure

10. strepiroteach = reproach

10.1 Finding Meaning

1. blithe	2. garish	3. rave
4. skirmish	5. flaunt	6. reproach
7. obscure	8. verity	9. absurd
10. lyric		

10.2 True or False

1. F	2. F	3. T
4. F	5. F	6. T
7. F	8. F	9. T
10. T		

10.3 Parts of Speech

Answers may vary depending on how the student uses the word, but generally the words are identified as the following parts of speech.

1. absurd—adjective	2. blithe—adjective
3. flaunt—verb	4. garish—adjective
5. lyric—adjective	6. obscure—adjective, noun, verb
7. rave—verb, adjective	8. reproach—verb, noun
9. skirmish—noun, verb	10. verity—noun

10.4 Antonyms and Synonyms

Antonym	Word	Synonym
truce	skirmish	Answer will vary.
hide	flaunt	Answer will vary.
not poetic	lyric	Answer will vary.
inaccuracy	verity	Answer will vary.
logical	absurd	Answer will vary.
keep quiet	rave	Answer will vary.
sorrowful	blithe	Answer will vary.
compliment	reproach	Answer will vary.
clear	obscure	Answer will vary.
drab	garish	Answer will vary.

10.5 Test

Part A

1. blithe	2. rave	3. skirmish
4. verity	5. garish	6. reproach
7. absurd	8. obscure	9. flaunt
10. lyric		

Part B

Original sentences will vary.

11.1 Unlocking the Mystery

1. schoondornest = condone

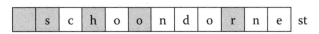

2. irripepriestser = repress

3. paslucecrumobly = succumb

4. efferungealine = frugal

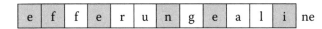

5. baberatzennels = brazen

6. aliarussthernes = austere

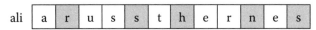

7. wespilancraters = placate

8. gaperuxdernents = prudent

9. rivteritentexer = vertex

10. rhinetrainguess = intrigue

11.1 Finding Meaning

1. placate	2. intrigue	3. succumb
4. frugal	5. austere	6. prudent
7. brazen	8. vertex	9. condone
10. repress		

11.2 True or False

1. F	2. T	3. F
4. T	5. T	6. T
7. F	8. F	9. F
10. F		

11.3 Parts of Speech

Answers may vary depending on how the students uses the word, but generally the words are identified as the following parts of speech.

1. austere—adjective	2. brazen—adjective
3. condone—verb	4. frugal—adjective
5. intrigue—verb, noun	6. placate—verb
7. prudent—adjective	8. repress—verb
9. succumb—verb	10. vertex—noun

11.4 Antonyms and Synonyms

Antonym	Word	Synonym
provoke	placate	Answer will vary.
resist	succumb	Answer will vary.
wasteful	frugal	Answer will vary.
meek	brazen	Answer will vary.
careless	prudent	Answer will vary.
bore	intrigue	Answer will vary.
bottom	vertex	Answer will vary.
let go	repress	Answer will vary.
adorned	austere	Answer will vary.
forbid	condone	Answer will vary.

11.5 Test

Part A

1. intrigue
2. austere
3. placate
4. brazen
5. frugal
6. condone
7. vertex
8. repress
9. succumb
10. prudent

Part B

1. placate
2. condone
3. vertex
4. brazen
5. prudent
6. intrigue
7. frugal
8. succumb
9. austere
10. repress

12.1 Unlocking the Mystery

1. gagaguachaires = gauche

2. sapriolinfixic = prolific

3. ghasitruthsens = astute

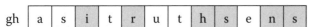

4. eldrilingernot = diligent

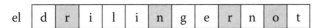

5. bestearinkers = stark

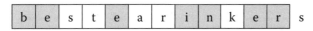

6. pasithorileakin = shriek

7. accusurtstorys = cursory

8. trunkrouslyst = unruly

9. prinsecinteller = incite

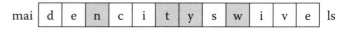

10. maidencityswivels = decisive

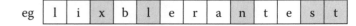

12.1 Finding Meaning

1. decisive
2. gauche
3. incite
4. prolific
5. unruly
6. astute
7. cursory
8. diligent
9. shriek
10. stark

12.2 True or False

1. F
2. F
3. T
4. F
5. T
6. F
7. T
8. T
9. F
10. F

12.3 Parts of Speech

Answers may vary depending on how the student uses the word, but generally the words are identified as the following parts of speech.

1. astute—adjective
2. cursory—adjective
3. decisive—adjective
4. diligent—adjective
5. gauche—adjective
6. incite—verb
7. prolific—adjective
8. shriek—verb, noun
9. stark—adjective
10. unruly—adjective

12.4 Antonyms and Synonyms

Antonym	Word	Synonym
ornate	stark	Answer will vary.
lazy	diligent	Answer will vary.
murmur	shriek	Answer will vary.
naïve	astute	Answer will vary.
thorough	cursory	Answer will vary.
obedient	unruly	Answer will vary.
tasteful	gauche	Answer will vary.
discourage	incite	Answer will vary.
unproductive	prolific	Answer will vary.
uncertain	decisive	Answer will vary.

12.5 Test

Part A

1. incite
2. decisive
3. diligent
4. unruly
5. stark
6. astute
7. shriek
8. gauche
9. prolific
10. cursory

Part B

Definitions will vary

13.1 Unlocking the Mystery

1. eglixblerantest = liberate

eg | l | i | x | b | l | e | r | a | n | t | e | s | t

13.1 Unlocking the Mystery, continued

2. staffordgotten = forge

st | a | f | f | o | r | d | g | o | t | t | e | n |

3. plesourepanses = surpass

ple | s | o | u | r | e | p | a | n | s | e | s |

4. trexapredaiters = expedite

t | r | e | x | a | p | r | e | d | a | i | t | e | r | s

5. irrespollutrents = resolute

i | r | r | e | s | p | o | l | l | u | t | r | e | n | ts

6. scorntrailteller = contrite

s | c | o | r | n | t | r | a | i | l | t | e | l | ler

7. applagliaraized = plagiarize

a | p | p | l | a | g | l | i | a | r | a | i | z | e | d

8. pippencathanites = penchant

pi | p | p | e | n | c | a | t | h | a | n | i | t | e | s

9. cyclopsinourset = copious

cy | c | l | o | p | s | i | n | o | u | r | s | e | t

10. gravitasidolly = avid

| g | r | a | v | i | t | a | s | i | d | o | l | ly

13.1 Finding Meaning

1. surpass	2. forge	3. resolute
4. expedite	5. penchant	6. copious
7. plagiarize	8. contrite	9. avid
10. liberate		

13.2 True or False

1. F	2. T	3. F
4. F	5. T	6. T
7. F	8. T	9. T
10. F		

13.3 Parts of Speech

Answers may vary depending on how the student uses the word, but the words are generally identified as the following parts of speech.

1. avid—adjective	2. contrite—adjective
3. copious—adjective	4. expedite—verb
5. forge—verb, noun	6. liberate—verb
7. penchant—noun	8. plagiarize—verb
9. resolute—adjective	10. surpass—verb

13.4 Antonyms and Synonyms

Antonym	Word	Synonym
originate	plagiarize	Answer will vary.
scarce	copious	Answer will vary.
indifferent	avid	Answer will vary.
lag behind	surpass	Answer will vary.
undetermined	resolute	Answer will vary.
unremorseful	contrite	Answer will vary.
aversion	penchant	Answer will vary.
demolish	forge	Answer will vary.
enslave	liberate	Answer will vary.
hinder	expedite	Answer will vary.

13.5 Test

Part A

1. expedite	2. copious	3. penchant
4. avid	5. contrite	6. forge
7. surpass	8. liberate	9. resolute
10. plagiarize		

Part B

1. forge	2. contrite	3. penchant
4. avid	5. liberate	6. copious
7. surpass	8. expedite	9. plagiarize
10. resolute		

14.1 Unlocking the Mystery

1. pajelosparndeys = jeopardy

pa | j | e | l | o | s | p | a | r | n | d | e | y | s

2. rainfruprigates = infuriate

ra | i | n | f | r | u | p | r | i | g | a | t | e | s

3. smeddelsuddems = delude

sm | e | d | d | e | l | s | u | d | d | e | m | s

4. presidionauntry = resonant

p | r | e | s | i | d | i | o | n | a | u | n | t | ry

5. michonytreatry = contrary

mi | c | h | o | n | y | t | r | e | a | t | r | y

6. tomertcutrinally = mercurial

to | m | e | r | t | c | u | t | r | i | n | a | l | ly

7. experitionrents = pertinent

ex | p | e | r | i | t | i | o | n | r | e | n | t | s

8. farmingwarblers = amiable

f | a | r | m | i | n | g | w | a | r | b | l | e | rs

9. ebayboyscoutty = boycott

10. bestegareglaten = segregate

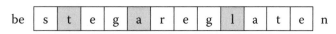

14.1 Finding Meaning

1. delude	2. jeopardy	3. mercurial
4. amiable	5. segregate	6. resonant
7. pertinent	8. boycott	9. contrary
10. infuriate		

14.2 True or False

1. F	2. F	3. T
4. T	5. F	6. F
7. T	8. F	9. T
10. F		

14.3 Parts of Speech

Answers may vary depending on how the student uses the word, but generally the words are identified as the following parts of speech.

1. amiable—adjective	2. boycott—verb or noun
3. contrary—adjective, noun	4. delude—verb
5. infuriate—verb	6. jeopardy—noun
7. mercurial—adjective	8. pertinent—adjective
9. resonant—adjective	10. segregate—verb

14.4 Antonyms and Synonyms

Antonym	Word	Synonym
soothe	infuriate	Answer will vary.
irrelevant	pertinent	Answer will vary.
support	boycott	Answer will vary.
unvarying	mercurial	Answer will vary.
unite	segregate	Answer will vary.
agreeble	contrary	Answer will vary.
antisocial	amiable	Answer will vary.
be truthful	delude	Answer will vary.
quiet	resonant	Answer will vary.
security	jeopardy	Answer will vary.

14.5 Test

Part A

1. segregate	2. boycott	3. jeopardy
4. delude	5. pertinent	6. infuriate
7. resonant	8. contrary	9. mercurial
10. amiable		

Part B

Original sentences will vary.

15.1 Unlocking the Mystery

1. pedestreetread = deter

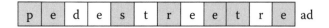

2. addivilsivatend = divisive

3. prexionearapter = exonerate

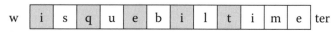

4. wisquebiltimeter = sublime

5. crabbyscounders = abscond

6. tearsevenersell = revere

7. shinstegarcitylad = integrity

8. nannanomaulyste = anomaly

9. equentiverailman = unveil

10. annexotophyates = neophyte

15.1 Finding Meaning

1. revere	2. abscond	3. neophyte
4. anomaly	5. integrity	6. exonerate
7. divisive	8. sublime	9. deter
10. unveil		

15.2 True or False

1. F	2. T	3. F
4. T	5. T	6. F
7. F	8. F	9. T
10. F		

15.3 Parts of Speech

Answers may vary depending on how the student uses the word, but generally the words are identified as the following parts of speech.

1. abscond—verb	2. anomaly—noun
3. deter—verb	4. divisive—adjective
5. exonerate—verb	6. integrity—noun
7. neophyte—noun	8. revere—verb
9. sublime—adjective	10. unveil—verb

15.4 Antonyms and Synonyms

Antonym	Word	Synonym
conceal	unveil	Answer will vary.
lowly	sublime	Answer will vary.
encourage	deter	Answer will vary.
expert	neophyte	Answer will vary.
dishonesty	integrity	Answer will vary.
condemn	exonerate	Answer will vary.
causing agreement	divisive	Answer will vary.
despise	revere	Answer will vary.
regularity	anomaly	Answer will vary.
remain	abscond	Answer will vary.

15.5 Test

Part A

1. divisive
2. revere
3. unveil
4. deter
5. integrity
6. neophyte
7. sublime
8. abscond
9. exonerate
10. anomaly

Part B

1. deter
2. integrity
3. neophyte
4. revere
5. divisive
6. unveil
7. exonerate
8. anomaly
9. abscond
10. sublime

Weekly Word Lists

Unit 1	Unit 2	Unit 3	Unit 4	Unit 5
abroad	acrid	abject	elude	adroit
baleful	candid	acute	forte	bolster
chasten	degrade	deluge	gaunt	dilate
edify	entail	envelop	impede	exploit
fervent	lenient	foible	kindle	mingle
inept	mitigate	futile	lucid	peril
lofty	pact	mollify	malign	prose
municipal	recoil	recluse	overt	scoff
pedigree	skeptic	subtle	staid	trifle
premise	vilify	tawdry	vogue	verbose

Unit 6	Unit 7	Unit 8	Unit 9	Unit 10
aloof	abhor	amend	akin	absurd
endorse	covert	belie	bias	blithe
hinder	emulate	deplete	concise	flaunt
innate	exalt	earnest	elicit	garish
lucent	hardy	morose	hallow	lyric
obtuse	leeway	placid	oust	obscure
poise	nuance	rapport	profuse	rave
subdue	recant	sheen	remit	reproach
terse	sustain	usurp	scorn	skirmish
urbane	tedium	wrath	veto	verity

Vocabulary Ladders © Prufrock Press Inc. This page may be photocopied or reproduced with permission for student use.

Unit 11	Unit 12	Unit 13	Unit 14	Unit 15
austere	astute	avid	amiable	abscond
brazen	cursory	contrite	boycott	anomaly
condone	decisive	copious	contrary	deter
frugal	diligent	expedite	delude	divisive
intrigue	gauche	forge	infuriate	exonerate
placate	incite	liberate	jeopardy	integrity
prudent	prolific	penchant	mercurial	neophyte
repress	shriek	plagiarize	pertinent	revere
succumb	stark	resolute	resonant	sublime
vertex	unruly	surpass	segregate	unveil

1. abhor
2. abject
3. abroad
4. abscond
5. absurd
6. acrid
7. acute
8. adroit
9. akin
10. aloof
11. amend
12. amiable
13. anomaly
14. astute
15. austere
16. avid
17. baleful
18. belie
19. bias
20. blithe
21. bolster
22. boycott
23. brazen
24. candid
25. chasten
26. concise
27. condone
28. contrary
29. contrite
30. copious
31. covert
32. cursory
33. decisive
34. degrade
35. delude
36. deluge
37. deplete
38. deter
39. dilate
40. diligent
41. divisive
42. earnest
43. edify
44. elicit
45. elude
46. emulate
47. endorse
48. entail
49. envelop
50. exalt
51. exonerate
52. expedite
53. exploit
54. fervent
55. flaunt
56. foible
57. forge
58. forte
59. frugal
60. futile
61. garish
62. gauche
63. gaunt
64. hallow
65. hardy
66. hinder
67. impede
68. incite
69. inept
70. infuriate
71. innate
72. integrity
73. intrigue
74. jeopardy
75. kindle
76. leeway
77. lenient
78. liberate
79. lofty
80. lucent
81. lucid
82. lyric
83. malign
84. mercurial
85. mingle
86. mitigate
87. mollify
88. morose
89. municipal
90. neophyte
91. nuance
92. obscure
93. obtuse
94. oust
95. overt
96. pact
97. pedigree
98. penchant
99. peril
100. pertinent
101. placate
102. placid
103. plagiarize
104. poise
105. premise
106. profuse
107. prolific
108. prose
109. prudent
110. rapport
111. rave
112. recant
113. recluse
114. recoil
115. remit
116. repress
117. reproach
118. resolute
119. resonant
120. revere
121. scoff
122. scorn
123. segregate
124. sheen
125. shriek
126. skeptic
127. skirmish
128. staid
129. stark
130. subdue
131. sublime
132. subtle
133. succumb
134. surpass
135. sustain
136. tawdry
137. tedium
138. terse
139. trifle
140. unruly
141. unveil
142. urbane
143. usurp
144. verbose
145. verity
146. vertex
147. veto
148. vilify
149. vogue
150. wrath